Japanese Religion: Unity and Diversity

Second Edition

H. BYRON EARHART

Western Michigan University

DICKENSON PUBLISHING COMPANY, INC.

Encino, California and Belmont, California

BOOKS BY THE SAME AUTHOR

Religion in the Japanese Experience: Sources and Interpretations
(Dickenson)

The New Religions of Japan: A Bibliography of Western-Language Materials
(Sophia University)

A Religious Study of the Mount Haguro Sect of Shugendo
(Sophia University)

The author is indebted to the following for permission to reprint copyrighted material: Sir George B. Sansom and Stanford University Press, for use of material from *A History of Japan;* Masaharu Anesaki and Charles E. Tuttle Company, for use of material from *History of Japanese Religion.*

ISBN-0-8221-0123-8
Library of Congress Catalog Card Number: 73-93288

Printed in the United States of America
Printing (last digit): 9 8 7 6 5 4 3

Table of Contents

Part II
THE DEVELOPMENT AND ELABORATION OF JAPANESE RELIGION

Part III
FOSSILIZATION AND RENEWAL IN JAPANESE RELIGION

TABLE OF CONTENTS

Foreword

THE RELIGIOUS LIFE OF MAN series is intended as an introduction to a large, complex field of inquiry—man's religious experience. It seeks to present the depth and richness of religious concepts, forms of worship, spiritual practices, and social institutions found in the major religious traditions throughout the world.

As a specialist in the languages and cultures in which a religion is found, each author is able to illuminate the meanings of a religious perspective and practice as other human beings have experienced it. To communicate this meaning to readers who have had no special training in these cultures and religions, the authors have attempted to provide clear, nontechnical descriptions and interpretations of religious life.

Different interpretive approaches have been used, depending upon the nature of the religious data; some religious expressions, for instance, lend themselves more to developmental, others more to topical studies. But this lack of a single interpretation may itself be instructive, for the experiences and practices regarded as religious in one culture may not be the most important in another.

THE RELIGIOUS LIFE OF MAN is concerned with, on the one hand, the variety of religious expressions found in different traditions and, on the other, the similarities in the structures of religious life. The various forms are interpreted in terms of their cultural context and historical continuity, demonstrating both the diverse expressions and commonalities of religious traditions. Besides the single volumes on different religions, the series offers a core book on the study of religious meaning, which describes different study approaches and examines several modes and structures of religious awareness. In addition, each book presents a list of materials for further reading, including translations of religious texts and detailed examinations of specific topics.

We hope the reader will find these volumes "introductory" in the most significant sense: an introduction to a new perspective for understanding himself and others.

Frederick J. Streng
Series Editor

Preface

I AM GRATEFUL for the opportunity to revise and enlarge this book, an opportunity made possible by the widespread use of the original edition. Since writing the first edition, I was able to make a brief research trip to Japan in 1969. Again, traditional Japanese hospitality provided more than ample reason to renew the earlier dedication of this book to our Japanese friends.

Writing *Japanese Religion* was my first publishing venture, and as on most maiden voyages, it was easier to determine the final goal than to steer a steady course to that goal. I tried to present an overall view of Japanese religion in its historical and dynamic unity, but hindsight shows that this attempt was not so successful as it may have been. Several colleagues and friendly critics have helped me reconsider those broad generalizations that tend to creep into a first book. Special thanks go to those who reviewed the first edition or manuscript of the second edition: Theodore M. Ludwig of Valparaiso University, Charles Wei-hsun Fu of Temple University, Alan L. Miller, and Dr. Frederick J. Streng of Southern Methodist University, editor of the Religious Life of Man series. Students have also suggested, by their pointed questions, need for clarification in the text. The fact that teachers and students have found the book helpful in understanding Japanese religion, in spite of these shortcomings, has encouraged me to undertake this revised edition.

Essentially the book has the same overall framework, with some sections rewritten for clarity and elaboration. A separate chapter is devoted to folk religion, in order to define more clearly this important but elusive aspect of Japanese religion. A chapter on the New Religions has been added to give better coverage to recent developments. Footnotes have been moved to the bottom of each page for easier reference; both the Selected Readings and Annotated Bibliography have been updated. Now that the companion sourcebook, *Religion in the Japanese Experience,* has been published, I feel that students have a better basis for evaluating the generalizations that are necessary in a brief introductory work such as this.

H. Byron Earhart
Western Michigan University

Preface to First Edition

ANYONE WHO STUDIES Japanese religion is amazed at the number of separate religions and the range of religious expression to be found in this chain of islands. There are ancient, prehistoric forms of religion as well as the so-called New Religions of recent emergence. There are unorganized forms of folk religion as well as profound systems of symbol and doctrine. Sometimes individual religious traditions are recognized as folk religion, Shinto, Buddhism, Confucianism, religious Taoism, and Christianity. These individual religious traditions, in turn, can be subdivided into particular folk religious practices, schools of Shinto, sects of Buddhism, schools of Confucianism, various forms of religious Taoism, and branches of Christianity.

The panorama of religion in Japan is truly bewildering. When I first began studying Japanese religion I was not only amazed but also confused by this panorama. I read many monographs on Japanese mythology, Shinto, folk religion, Buddhism, New Religions, and other topics, but usually these topics are treated in isolation from each other. Therefore, even after reading many scholarly works, I could not understand how all these separate fragments could form the total picture of Japanese religion. I felt as if I were in a butcher shop looking at all the different cuts of beef, trying to understand what a cow is.

Now, after several years of specialized research in Japan (and after several years of lecturing on the religions of Japan), I am no less impressed by the diversity and complexity of Japanese religion. At the same time, I am convinced that the only way we can understand this diversity and complexity is by interpreting these many elements in their historical relationships with each other. Although this book is introductory in nature, it aims at a unified interpretation of Japanese religious history which is lacking in most treatments of Japanese religion.

Japanese Religion has the twofold purpose of presenting the general reader and teacher with an introduction to the religions of Japan in the context of their historical unity. It will be of interest to all general readers who are interested in either Japanese studies or religious studies. It is conceived and written as an introduction to the history of religion in Japan, and can be read as a first book in this area. No technical knowledge of Japanese history, Japanese religion, or the Japanese language is required for understanding the material.* The author hopes that it will also be of use to more advanced students and teachers, who are acquainted with one area of Japanese history and culture but look for a general understanding of religion in Japan. Whereas general readers may use the book as a stepping stone (through the Selected Readings and Annotated Bibliography) to a deeper understanding of Japanese religion, advanced students and teachers may use it as a unified context in which they can integrate their specialized readings.

I would like to acknowledge above all the help of former teachers and of fellowship aid, which was indispensable in the preliminary research for this book. Thanks are offered to Professors Mircea Eliade, Charles Long, and Joseph M. Kitagawa of The University of Chicago for affording me insights into the history of religions. To Professor Edwin McClellan, also of The University of Chicago, I am indebted for Japanese language training. To Professor Ichiro Hori of Tohoku University and Tokyo University I express special thanks for guiding my research in Japan, 1962–65.

A National Defense Foreign Language Fellowship at The University of Chicago, 1960–62, and at Columbia University, summer, 1962, enabled me to combine Japanese language study with a Ph.D. program. A Fulbright fellowship from the United States Educational Commission in Japan financed my dissertation research at Tohoku University, Sendai, Japan, 1962–65.

A number of students, friends, and colleagues have kindly read earlier drafts of the manuscript and made suggestions for improvement. Professor Kitagawa kindly read and criticized the manuscript before the final revision. Several drafts of the manuscript were typed by the secretarial staff of Vanderbilt University and Western Michigan University. Editorial help was given by Mr. Richard J. Trudgen, President, Dickenson Publishing Company, and Professor Frederick J. Streng, editor of THE RELIGIOUS LIFE OF MAN series.

During the three years 1962–65, my family and I enjoyed Japanese hospitality at Sendai, where we made our home, and wherever we traveled throughout Japan. To our Japanese friends, who made our stay so pleasantly profitable, this book is dedicated.

H. Byron Earhart

---

*All markings for long vowels have been omitted; no publications in Japanese are cited. Reference to Japanese names follows the Japanese usage of giving the family name first.

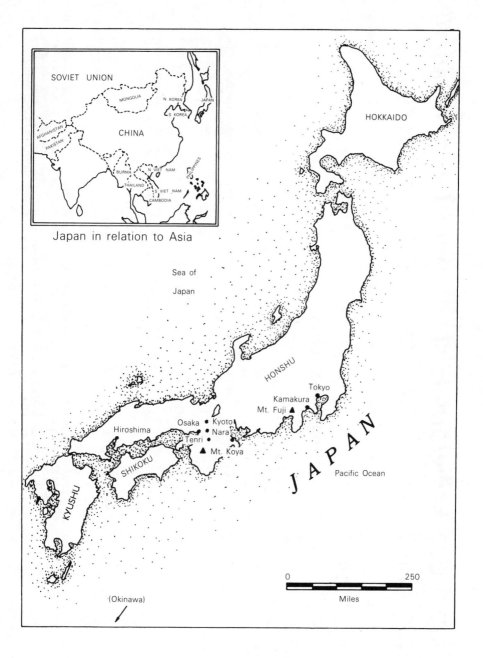

SOVIET UNION

MONGOLIA

N KOREA
JAPAN
S. KOREA

AFGHANISTAN
PAKISTAN

CHINA

BURMA
N VIET NAM
PHILIPPINES
THAILAND
S VIET NAM
CAMBODIA

Japan in relation to Asia

Sea of

Japan

HOKKAIDO

HONSHU

Tokyo
Kamakura
Mt. Fuji ▲

Osaka ● Kyoto
Hiroshima
Nara
Tenri ●
▲ Mt. Koya

JAPAN

SHIKOKU

Pacific Ocean

KYUSHU

0   250

Miles

(Okinawa)

Table of Japanese Religious History, with Chronological Periods and Corresponding Cultural Features

(For a more complete account, see "A Chronological Table of Religious Affairs in Japan," pp. 467–77 in *Religious Studies in Japan*.)

(Chronology in Japanese Historical Periods)	(Economic, Social, and Political Features)	(Religious Events and Characteristics)
	I. FORMATIVE PERIOD	
Jomon ⎫ Prehistoric and Proto- Yayoi ⎬ historic (to sixth Kofun ⎭ century A.D.)	Hunting and gathering culture gives way to rice agriculture and more sedentary, small village organization; increasing centralization around leading clans	Indigenous Japanese tradition: agricultural festivals, reverence for the dead, divine descent of the imperial line, clan as the religious unit
Taika (645–710)	Influx of Chinese culture marks Japan's first contact with a literate and highly organized culture; the first truly centralized government, patterned after Chinese models (such as legal codes)	Importation of foreign traditions: Buddhism, Confucianism, religious Taoism; Shinto organized from the indigenous traditions; earliest interaction of these traditions
Nara (710–784)	First permanent capital; elaborate life at the imperial court and among the nobility, widely separated from the common farmer; first Japanese writings, including dynastic chronicles and *Manyoshu*	Six philosophical schools of Buddhism; system of provincial temples with Todaiji at Nara as the central cathedral; further interaction of the native tradition with Buddhism and Taoism
	II. PERIOD OF DEVELOPMENT AND ELABORATION	
Heian (794–1185)	Capital moved to Kyoto; highly developed aesthetic life among court and nobility; *Tale of Genji*, the world's first novel; increasing importance of feudal estates and the warrior class; Mongol invasions of 1274 and 1281	Buddhist sects of Shingon and Tendai founded, dominate Heian period; Buddhism becomes more closely related to Japanese culture and begins to penetrate the countryside; Shinto becomes more highly organized; *Engishiki* compiled 927

Period		
Kamakura (1185–1333)	Military dictator controls political power (emperor is secluded at Kyoto); real seat of government moves to Kamakura; attention shifts from the effeminate nobleman to the powerful warrior; rise of the merchant class; growing sense of uncertainty with increased civil strife	Buddhist sects of Pure Land, Nichiren, and Zen founded, dominate Kamakura period; Buddhism enters the life of the common people and spreads throughout the land; development of highly eclectic medieval Shinto; thorough blending of these traditions
Muromachi (1333–1568) and Momoyama (1568–1600)	Great civil strife; expansion and development of agricultural lands and techniques; growth of towns and markets; blending of the culture of warriors and noblemen; greater unification of the country under the military ruler, subjugation of religious headquarters to political authority; first major contact with the West	Kitabatake writes in support of the supremacy of the imperial line (1339); crystallization of sect and denominational lines; St. Francis Xavier and introduction of Christianity (sixteenth century)

III. PERIOD OF FOSSILIZATION AND RENEWAL

Period		
Tokugawa (1600–1867)	Widespread peace and stability under supreme control of the military dictator; expulsion of Christianity and "closed door" policy limiting foreign access to Japan; dominance of merchant class; cities grow in size and importance; rise of popular arts such as woodblock prints and novels	Christianity proscribed; Buddhism made a branch of the state; Neo-Confucianism made the rationale of the state; Shinto overshadowed by Buddhism but developing rationale for separation from Buddhism; first appearance of the New Religions; secularism expressed in popular arts
Meiji (1868–1911) Taisho (1912–1925) Showa (1926–) } Modern (1868–1945)	Transition from feudal to modern period; military dictator steps down while emperor is formally made head of state; feudal state is abolished and modern nation-state established with centralized authority at Tokyo; remarkable educational and industrial achievements; three major wars: Sino-Japanese (1894–95), Russo-Japanese (1904–05), World War II (1937–1945)	Buddhism disestablished; Shinto established as state religion; ban on Christianity lifted; Catholicism reintroduced and Protestantism introduced for the first time; all traditions become nationalistic; more New Religions appear
Postwar (after 1945)	Allied occupation 1945–52 marks Japan's first major defeat and occupation of her territory; prewar nationalism and militaristic control give way to greater liberty, and tendency toward "democracy" and internationalism; remarkable rebuilding of Japan's cities and industrial facilities; Japan emerges as a major economic and political force in Asia	Shinto disestablished; complete religious freedom; general demoralization and disorganization among the older religions, with gradual recovery and reorganization; New Religions the most conspicuous religious activity; religious indifference and secularism widespread

1.

Introduction to Japanese Religion

Japan: A Living Museum of Religions

The many separate religions and the range of religious expressions found in Japan constitute a "living museum of religions." Here one finds prehistoric and indigenous religious roots together with several foreign traditions that have been remolded into a distinctive Japanese religious tradition. Often these different dimensions of Japanese religion have been classified according to the individual traditions, such as folk religion, Shinto, Buddhism, religious Taoism, and Confucianism. Indeed, most Western writers have chosen to dissect Japanese religion into its individual components and compartmentalize each element. Although compartmentalization may be much simpler for the writer, the artificial separation of these traditions not only distorts the individual elements but also prevents the reader from gaining a total picture of Japanese religion.

None of these traditions remained a pure form in isolation, so they cannot be clearly separated into mutually exclusive notions of indigenous and foreign traditions. Even Shinto cannot be considered as simply indigenous to Japan. The very term "Shinto" was borrowed from the Chinese, and as an organized religion Shinto borrowed heavily from both Buddhist and Chinese traditions. On the other hand, neither Buddhism nor the Chinese traditions (Confucianism and Taoism) can be considered as purely foreign in character. Both Buddhism and the Chinese traditions took on a decidedly Japanese character. The various traditions became so deeply rooted in Japanese life, that the ordinary villager considers every aspect of local religion as indigenous to his village.

Likewise, these traditions cannot be treated as distinct from one another. For example, folk religion in Japan draws on indigenous traditions and popular elements from Buddhism and Chinese traditions; in turn, folk religion has interacted with the popular aspects of Shinto, Buddhism, and Confucianism. The religious traditions do not have separate histories, for they are not separated in Japanese religious life. It is well known that the same Japanese person can be affiliated with most of these traditions at the same time. Often one is married in a Shinto shrine and buried in a Buddhist temple. He may participate in unorganized folk religious practices, and many of his notions about lucky and unlucky may hark back to religious Taoism. Not conflicting with this, his ethical convictions may be Confucian in character. Therefore, we can best understand the wholeness of Japanese religion by studying its elements in historical relationship to each other.

There is no single organized religion called "Japanese religion," at least not in the same sense in which we refer to the Christian religion. On the contrary, by using the notion of the unity of Japanese religion we emphasize the historical plane in which the individual traditions are naturally related. Therefore, the book is not divided into separate topics such as Buddhism, Shinto, Confucianism, and so on. Instead, the various religious traditions are treated in their interaction with each other in the important historical eras. This approach raises methodological questions which have been treated elsewhere.[1] The methodological problem of dealing with the long history of a complex tradition is, of course, not unique to Japan. In fact, neighboring China presents a similar case.

The structure of this book demonstrates the historical viewpoint to be followed in interpreting Japanese religion. There are three major periods that provide a historical context in which to discuss the religious traditions of Japan. These three historical periods define the stage on which the various religious traditions act out in unison the panoramic drama of Japanese religion. We might say that the first period (prehistory to ninth century A.D.) sets the stage for the formation of Japanese religion, since in this initial period the most important religious traditions all make their appearance. In the second period (ninth to seventeenth centuries) these religious traditions work out the development and elaboration of Japanese religion both in terms of mutual influence and independent organization. The third period (seventeenth century to present) portrays the tendency of the various traditions toward stagnation and excessive formalization, which in turn stimulates several kinds of renewal. This brings us down to the present, where we must wait for the next act in the unending drama of Japanese religion. Religious history does not end with this third period, but will be continued and transformed in future events.

Unity and Plurality in Japanese Religion

One way of viewing the whole of Japanese religious history is in terms of unity and plurality. That is, a plurality of religious traditions is found in the overall unity of a common cultural and religious context. A distinctive feature of Japanese religious history is that there exists a number of separate religious traditions, such as Shinto, Buddhism, and Confucianism, and that the individual, rather than belonging exclusively to one of them, is consciously affiliated with, or unconsciously participates in, several of them. With the important exceptions of the Jodo Shin sect and the Nichiren tradition, no Japanese tradition has claimed

---

[1]See H. Byron Earhart, "Toward a Unified Interpretation of Japanese Religion." (Complete publication information is given in footnotes only for works which do not appear in the Annotated Bibliography.)

absolute truth to the exclusion of all other traditions. (Christianity in Japan also has made a claim to absolute truth, but not as a Japanese tradition.) Traditionally, a person participated in all five of the formative traditions at different moments of his life. A Japanese person found religious fulfillment not in one tradition alone but in the sacred power expressed by all five traditions as a whole. In other words, Japanese traditions tend to be mutually syncretistic, rather than mutually exclusive.

Unity and Diversity in Japanese Religion

Another way of viewing this religious history is in terms of unity and diversity. Within the unity of a single religious tradition, a great diversity of religious attitudes may find expression. For example, Buddhism and Shinto include, within their traditions, the full spectrum of religious expression, from the most popular belief to the most abstract philosophy. Thus, there are several levels of religiosity present simultaneously within a religious tradition.

In the face of this diversity, the individual finds unity by participating at a particular level in several different traditions. The uneducated person may resort to Shinto and Buddhism as well as folk religion for the same religious petition, with no sense of contradiction. Often both Shinto shrines and Buddhist temples distribute the same charms or administer the same blessings. This is unity on the popular level.

More highly educated persons may find satisfaction in the theoretical expressions of Buddhism, Shinto, Confucianism, and religious Taoism. In fact, Shinto and Buddhism were able to appropriate cosmological theories from religious Taoism and socio-moral theories from Confucianism. This represents unity on a more theoretical level. Thus, at a given level, a unity of religious attitude can extend across several separate traditions.

Unity and diversity within Japanese religion is also illustrated by the tension between local traditions and the national unity. In the earliest times there was a tension between loyalty to the clan priest-chief and loyalty to the imperial line. In later times this tension became expressed in the local diversification within both Shinto and Buddhism. The Shinto shrines especially pride themselves on their unique local rites and usages.

The extreme example of local diversity is in the realm of folk religion. Every region of Japan is proud of its special food products and folk crafts. Similarly, every region likes to boast of its unique festival or peculiar folk tale or old religious edifice. Often the ancient history and economy of the area are linked inseparably to its folk crafts and religious customs. Perhaps it is easier for Europeans than for Americans to understand this amazing diversity of local customs and the intense pride which goes with it. Nevertheless, this diversity strengthens rather than threatens the overall unity. For example, the great importance of local custom for Shinto shrines makes the shrines all the more esteemed by the surrounding people as a concrete example of their involvement in the long Japanese tradition. Such local customs increase rather than diminish the truly national traditions, such as reverence for the emperor.

SELECTED READINGS

Suggestions for further reading are listed at the end of each chapter, covering the topics described in that chapter. Complete publication information is given in the Annotated Bibliography.

Anesaki, Masaharu. *History of Japanese Religion.* A standard one-volume history published in 1930, valuable for its balanced treatment of the premodern period.

Bloom, Alfred. "Japan: Religion of a Sacred People in a Sacred Land." A concise summary of Shinto and Buddhism.

Earhart, H. Byron. *Religion in the Japanese Experience: Sources and Interpretations.* See this sourcebook for the original documents and more detailed scholarly works on which this general book is based.

_____. "Towards a Unified Interpretation of Japanese Religion." This article sets forth the methodological approach to the "unity and diversity" of Japanese religion as presented in this book.

Embree, John F. *Suye Mura.* See Chapter 7 for the interrelationships among the several religious traditions in Japan.

Kitagawa, Joseph M. *Religion in Japanese History.* The most up-to-date account of Japanese religion in a single volume, especially valuable for its treatment of the modern period.

Matsumoto, Shigeru. "Introduction," in *Japanese Religion,* edited by Ichiro Hori, pp. 11–27. A concise overview of religions in Japan.

2.

Persistent Themes in Japanese Religious History

The general unity of Japanese religion is evidenced by a nexus of persistent themes in Japanese religious history. Six themes are suggested here as representative, but of course not exhaustive, of the unity of Japanese religion.

One theme which runs through Japanese religious history is the closeness of man, gods, and nature. In this context "gods" can be understood as either the *kami* of Shinto or the Buddhas and *bodhisattvas* (Buddhist Divinities) of Buddhism. Because there is no exact English equivalent for the word *kami*, it will be used throughout the text without translation. The important thing to remember is that *kami* is much more inclusive than the English word "god." The notion of *kami* is elusive because of the great number of *kami* and their various forms. Many *kami* participated in the creation of the world and in a mythological age of specialized divinities not too different from the mythological world of ancient Greece and Rome. In addition to the *kami* of mythology, in ancient times as well as at present, natural objects, animals, and even human beings have been identified as *kami*. In fact, according to one of the greatest Shinto scholars, Motoori Norinaga (1730–1801), "In ancient usage, anything whatsoever which was outside the ordinary, which possessed superior power or which was awe-inspiring was called *kami*."[1] If they were considered powerful enough, "evil and mysterious things" also rated as *kami*, because the primary consideration was the power to inspire and not "goodness or meritorious deeds." The identity of *kami* is so elastic that perhaps the best general term for understanding *kami* is the notion of the sacred.[2]

Man is closely related to both *kami* and Buddhas. In fact, he can even rise to the status of a *kami* or Buddha. The emperor was considered to be a living *kami*, since he was a direct descendant of the *kami*. Other human beings can

---

[1]Quoted in Daniel C. Holtom, *The National Faith of Japan. A Study in Modern Shinto*, p. 23. For an excerpt from this work, see H. Byron Earhart, *Religion in the Japanese Experience*, pp. 9–13.

[2]Mircea Eliade has elaborated the notion of the sacred as a general feature of all religion, but dominant within cosmic religions. See his *The Sacred and the Profane. The Nature of Religion*. Translated by Willard R. Trask (New York: Harcourt, Brace and Company, 1959).

attain divinity, too. For example, the military ruler (*shogun*) Tokugawa Ieyasu was venerated as divine or semi-divine even during his lifetime (late sixteenth and early seventeenth centuries). The founders of Buddhist sects and especially the founders of the New Religions during the last two centuries also attained more or less divine status. In contrast with monotheistic religions such as Judaism and Christianity, Japanese religion emphasizes neither one sovereign God nor a sharp distinction between the several gods and man. Man and gods alike share in the beauty of nature. The Judaeo-Christian theological tendency is to think of a hierarchy with God first, man second, and nature a poor third. In Japanese religion the three are more on equal terms. Man, gods, and nature form a triangle of harmonious interrelationships. Agriculture and fishing are closely related to the rituals and festivals of Shinto shrines and Buddhist temples. Zen Buddhism in particular, together with Shinto, express a love of nature that makes them akin to the Taoist sentiments of China. The harmony between man, the gods, and nature is a cornerstone of Japanese religion.

A second theme of Japanese religious history is the crucial function of the family system, including both living and dead members. The dead are so important in Japanese religion that the label of ancestor worship has been applied to Japanese as well as to Chinese religion. Family unity and continuity are essential for carrying out the important rituals honoring the dead ancestors. Even beyond the family system, there is great religious significance in the dead, their burial or cremation, and periodic memorials. In fact, the dead can rise to the status of "gods." A dead person is referred to euphemistically as a Buddha (*hotoke*), and the tacit understanding is that after a fixed number of periodic memorials the dead person joins the company of ancestors as a kind of *kami*. Some shrines are dedicated to the spirits of famous men, such as the great Tokugawa ruler Ieyasu. At present, the religious function of most Buddhist priests and temples is to perform masses and memorials.

The family is important not only for revering ancestors but also for providing cohesion for religious activities. The home was formerly the center of religious devotion. Traditionally, every home featured a miniature shrine (sometimes called "god-shelf" or *kamidana*) for daily prayers. There was also a Buddhist altar (*butsudan*) for offerings to the family ancestors and periodic memorials. The *kamidana* are still found in many homes, especially in rural areas, but also are retained in such places as small shops and even in oceangoing ships. The *butsudan* are found in almost every home, even in the modern apartments where the *kamidana* are often missing. These family altars are not so ancient, representing an economic prosperity of later times, but they indicate the central religious function of the home. Other semi-religious seasonal activities (notably at New Year's) take place at the home. In ancient times the head of the clan was also a priest; in later times many shrines and temples were closely linked to specific families. It is not surprising that as Shinto and Buddhism became more highly organized they assumed the form of a hereditary priesthood. Japanese social as well as religious organization emphasizes a hierarchical ordering based on respect for elders.

A third theme found in Japanese religious history is the significance of purification, rituals, and charms. These religious elements are not unique to Japan, and in fact often represent borrowings from Indian and Chinese traditions, but they have become thoroughly integrated into the Japanese religious scene. In front of every Shinto shrine, water is provided for washing the hands and rinsing the mouth before approaching the shrine. The insistence on purification—both physical and spiritual—is still basic to Japanese religion. Formerly there were many prohibitions and purifications connected with such matters as death and menstruation. This emphasis on purity carries over into such contemporary customs as the hot bath, and the damp face cloth provided for guests. Purification rituals using salt, water, and fire—all considered to be purifying agents—are found in Buddhist, Shinto, and folk traditions. Other rituals take care of every conceivable human and spiritual need. Many rituals are connected with agriculture and fishing, in order to relate man, gods, and nature in a beneficial manner. Some rituals meet personal crises, such as sickness. The paper charms distributed by shrines and temples include a number of specific boons, like warding off fire, preventing or curing sickness, and other "practical" benefits. One of the most popular charms in modern times is for "traffic safety"—protection against car accidents. Even Buddhist scriptures (in Chinese translation) were recited as blessings, and phrases from the scriptures were memorized as semi-magical formulas. Taoistic charms and formulas crept into both Shinto and Buddhism, but Buddhism was the major source of popular prayers and magical formulas.

A fourth theme of Japanese religious history is the prominence of local festivals and individual cults. Buddhist temples and Shinto shrines are not the site of weekly services, as is the case with Christian churches, but this does not diminish their importance. Because periodic festivals are the expression of the whole village, or section of a large city, they are unifying forces which link the individual homes into a larger religious group. Often social and economic activities of small villages center around the Shinto shrine. The local festival with its carnival atmosphere is quite typical of Japanese religiosity. In this light we can understand the fact that in Japan the celebration of Christmas has become popular, even though Christianity in general has not prospered.

Individual cults, though not organized on a national scale, play a crucial role in religious devotion. The *bodhisattvas* of Buddhism, especially Jizo and Kannon, have claimed probably the largest following. Statues of these *bodhisattvas* are found in the villages or along the roadside as well as in temples, and they receive the devotion of all those who look to them for spiritual help. Usually priests play little or no role in these devotional cults. Ordinarily a small group of people will form a voluntary association (called *ko*) which meets regularly in the members' homes for devotion to one *bodhisattva*. Various *kami* (including gods of Indian and Chinese origin) are revered by groups of fishermen or other tradesmen. Often the existence of a flourishing cult of this kind at a shrine or temple accounts for most of its visitors and financial income.

A fifth theme within Japanese religious history is the way in which religion is woven into everyday life. This theme is simply another aspect of the previous four themes. The Japanese identification with gods and nature, the importance of the family, the significance of rituals and charms, and the prominence of individual cults—all lead religion into a natural and close relationship to everyday life. For example, even if there is no regular weekly attendance at Shinto shrines and Buddhist temples corresponding to the Judaeo-Christian sabbath, there are regular stages in an individual's life which take him to shrines and temples. Traditionally, the young infant was carried to the local Shinto shrine and presented to the guardian deity. In case of sickness or special need, one usually visited the shrine or temple which granted that specific blessing. Likewise, in recent times the traditional wedding often takes place in a Shinto shrine, and the funeral mass is performed (like the subsequent memorial celebrations) in a Buddhist temple.

Through both formal and informal means, religion has been specifically related to concrete economic activities. Some temples and shrines, for example, are oriented to the fishing communities in which they are found; they pray for large catches, safety on the sea, and repose for the drowned. Some saints are formally considered the patron figures of certain crafts. In an informal sense, many folk practices are inseparable from the various stages of rice cultivation. Religion even pervades the Japanese sense of humor. For example, the great Zen saint of China, Bodhidharma (who sat in meditation until his legs fell off), is remembered in Japan as the legless doll called Daruma who, as many times as he falls, always rights himself.

A sixth theme of Japanese religious history is the natural bond between Japanese religion and the Japanese nation. It is true that from the Meiji Restoration of 1868 until 1945 Japanese religion took on a nationalistic character which supported the state in its military campaigns. However, the close tie between Japanese religion and the nation at large is an indelible feature of Japanese history. It is as true of Buddhism as of Shinto, because Buddhism lent a hand in unifying and supporting the government. All the formative elements of Japanese religion have blended with and supported the national heritage. Indeed, this is partly what wove Buddhism, Confucianism (Neo-Confucianism), and religious Taoism into the warp and woof of Japanese religion.

SELECTED READINGS

Anesaki, Masaharu. *History of Japanese Religion.* See pp. 6–15 for general remarks on the nature of religion in Japan, as contrasted with religion in Western civilization.
Earhart, H. Byron. *Religion in the Japanese Experience.* See Part One for a general introduction to Japanese religion.
Kishimoto, Hideo. "The Meaning of Religion to the Japanese People." A comparison of Japanese and Western religion.
Nakamura, Hajime. *Ways of Thinking of Eastern Peoples.* The section on Japan, pp.

345–587, is the most complete treatment of the distinctive features of Japanese life and thought.

2. Themes in Japanese Religious History

Part I

THE FORMATION
OF JAPANESE
RELIGION

3.
The Earliest Religious Tradition in Japan

The Evidence and Meaning of the Earliest Religion in Japan

Our historical study of Japanese religion begins, quite logically, with the earliest known Japanese religion. Among the several traditions which constitute Japanese religion, the prehistoric heritage is of primary importance. The beginning of religion in Japan, like all other aspects of her early culture, is not well known. We do not know exactly where the Japanese people came from, just as we do not know how the Japanese language was formed. In the absence of certainty in these matters, there have arisen a number of theories which would account for the emergence of the culture and people of Japan. It is obvious that Japanese culture shows affinity to the culture of the north as well as to the culture of the south, but scholars disagree on the interpretation of this affinity. Some have favored a southern hypothesis, seeing the ultimate source of the Japanese tradition in the Ryukyu Islands and farther south. Others have emphasized a northern hypothesis, seeing the main contribution to Japanese culture enter from the Asian continent via Korea. Future research will have to take into account both hypotheses.

Several aspects of prehistoric Japan are important for understanding her earliest (and even later) religion. In the first place, man seems to be a comparatively recent arrival to Japan, especially compared to her neighbor, China. Some of the oldest human remains and oldest evidence for religion (religious burial), some hundreds of thousands of years old, have been excavated in China. By contrast, geologists and archaeologists are still discussing the evidence for a Paleolithic (old stone age) culture in Japan. This means that there was perhaps never a pure hunting culture in Japan. The decisive evidence for early man in

Japan places him in the Neolithic age (c. 10,000 B.C.). He lived in a hunting and gathering or hunting and fishing economy. Therefore, the term "indigenous religion" must be applied to Japan only with the realization of its relatively shorter period of development, and of its mixed character. (By comparison, both India and China possessed complicated religious scriptures during the first millennium B.C. About the middle of the first millennium B.C. Buddha arose in India; in China both Confucius and Lao-tzu are dated from about the same time.)

Even in the beginning Japanese religion was a product of influence from several directions. Indeed, the geographical location of the Japanese islands is a clue to the formation of Japanese religion. Geographically, the Japanese islands have been in a good position to receive periodic influence from several directions. Especially the recurring influence from the Asian continent has played a crucial role in Japanese religious history. However, it is well to emphasize the periodic or recurring nature of the continental influence, because until recent times there was no constant contact with the mainland. The span of ocean between Japan and Asia was short enough to allow occasional voyages, but the difficulty of the voyage severely limited their frequency. Consequently, every Asian element which entered Japan was left to ferment in a somewhat isolated setting. This geographical condition is a major factor in the development of a truly Japanese religion. The only sense in which we can speak of an indigenous religion in Japan is to refer to the distinctive Japanese blending of several diverse components. The aim of Part I is to trace the various elements, prehistoric and historic, which contributed to the formation of a Japanese religion.

To understand the prehistoric contribution to Japanese religion, we have to synthesize the archaeological evidence which precedes written records. If the very earliest archaeological finds (possibly Paleolithic) are excluded, the bulk of this evidence falls into two prehistoric periods called the Jomon and the Yayoi, followed by a transitional period called Kofun which shades into early history. These three periods represent successive stages of culture which cannot be dated precisely. The Jomon period draws its name from distinctive pottery decoration (Jomon or "code pattern") which may have started as early as 6000 B.C. or as late as 3000 B.C., and continued until about 250 B.C. The main evidence for the culture of this period, usually considered Neolithic, is found in the many shell-heaps along the sea coast where men made shell-fish their main food. There is also some evidence for the existence of mountain dwellers who combined hunting and gathering activities. The Yayoi period is named after the district in Tokyo where a different style of pottery was found. The approximate dates 250 B.C. to 250 A.D. are usually associated with it. The major innovation of the Yayoi period is the cultivation of rice in paddies, utilizing the control of water. It seems that hunting and fishing were continued in addition to the new practice of growing rice. Kofun means "tomb," so the Kofun period is literally the Tomb period. Although the Yayoi period represents continental influence with the introduction of rice, the Kofun period marks the entrance of a highly defined Asian culture. The period, stretching from about 250 A.D. to 600 A.D., is named for the huge earthen

mausolea or tombs which were erected during this time. These elaborate mausolea were built only for the ruling class, and there is one school of thought which
conceives this ruling class as a conquering force which swept in from Asia with
horses and iron weapons.[1]

Another unanswered question of early history is the relationship of the Ainu
and their culture to the Japanese. The Ainu, who once occupied much of the main
island Honshu, were gradually driven east and north by the advancing Japanese,
and now survive mainly in Hokkaido. Racially the Ainu are Caucasian and have
much body hair; this places them in sharp contrast to the Japanese, who are
Mongolian and have less body hair. In physical appearance the Japanese are
distinguished by the fold of skin at the corner of the eye, which Westerners see
as a "slant eye." After the Yayoi period the Japanese depended heavily on rice
agriculture; the Ainu traditionally lived by hunting, fishing, and gathering.

At one time Western scholars thought that the Ainu were the forerunners
of the later Japanese, and tried to find the origin of Japanese language, culture,
and religion among the Ainu. Now scholars tend to see the Ainu more as an
isolated "pocket" of Caucasians in northeast Asia. For the Ainu are linked with
prehistoric northern Asia and Europe not only racially, but also by their most
important traditional ritual, the bear sacrifice. However, even if the story of the
Ainu does not solve the riddle of the early Japanese, there was a great deal of
interaction between the two traditions. Especially in northern Honshu and Hokkaido, place names are borrowed from the Ainu, and some places formerly sacred
to the Ainu have been taken over by the Japanese. One of the controversial factors
relating the religions of the two peoples is the similarity in the name for divinity
—*kami* in Japanese and *kamui* in Ainu language.

The reason for tracing all these prehistoric developments is that they contain
the earliest known religion in Japan, the foundation on which later religion is
based. In fact, it can be shown that certain religious themes continue from
prehistoric times up through the present. Due to the fragmentary character of the
evidence it is impossible to reconstruct the whole fabric of religion in these early
periods, but certain religious features are prominent. While one must recognize
the great diversity for different regions and different periods, there were various
religious expressions concerned with the dead and afterlife, fertility, and sacred
objects. Mythology, rituals, and religious organization can be inferred only by
ethnological comparison.

The Religious Significance of Burial and the Dead

Man has almost always shown a religious attitude toward the dead, since he
recognizes the passage from this physical life to another form of spiritual exis-

---

[1]John W. Hall supports the alternative argument for a "primitive feudalism" arising
on Japanese soil; see his *Japanese History. New Dimensions of Approach and Understanding,* p. 25.

tence. The early Japanese were no exception, for they practiced several types of burial for the dead. The first evidence of intentional burials is the simple burial of bodies in a flexed position, or together with red ochre and stones. During the Yayoi period there appeared the custom of interment in jars. This custom originated from Korea, and gradually the jars came to be covered with stone slabs (dolmen burial). This seems to have been the forerunner of the large mausolea called *kofun*. These mausolea or tombs are often huge mounds covering a stone chamber, all of which is surrounded by a moat. Boat-shaped coffins of wood and stone in the tombs may indicate the voyage of the soul to the next world. In general, with the passage of time, there was an increasing concern for the disposal of the dead. The transition to agriculture in Yayoi times probably led to a higher valuation of land and burial in the earth; the erection of tombs probably was the result of a more abrupt intrusion from the Asian continent.

How can we interpret all these concerns for the dead and afterlife? The initial Western scholarship on Japanese religion was confused in asking whether the origin of Japanese religion was ancestor worship or nature worship; there was also the confused controversy as to whether Japanese ancestor worship was truly indigenous or a Chinese importation.[2] But there is no single origin of Japanese religion. The evidence suggests that the Japanese people have always shown a reverent concern for the dead, and that this concern has assumed diverse forms, not only in prehistoric but also in historic times. Much of the archaeological evidence for understanding Japanese religion is found in burials, especially in the elaborate tomb burials of the Kofun period. In later periods the religious significance of the dead is expressed in Buddhist funeral and memorial services.

The Religious Significance of Fertility

From Jomon times on, objects are found which point to a connection of religion and fertility. Large stone clubs suggest a phallic symbol, while small clay figurines are probably symbols of fertility and protection. During the Yayoi period the figurines took on a definitely female form. Perhaps the burial of metal spears and bells (indicating the intrusion of continental metal-working techniques) was also linked to the notion of fertility. With the introduction of rice cultivation in Yayoi times we begin to see an increased emphasis on fertility which colors the agricultural and religious life of all later Japanese history. There was an annual ritual rhythm that linked religious ceremonies to every aspect of the growing and harvesting of rice.

Archaeology has turned up many sacred objects of prehistoric Japan, such as the phallic stone clubs and clay figurines already mentioned. However, three sacred objects are outstanding due to their importance in historic times: the *magatama* (comma-shaped jewels), swords, and mirrors. In later times a set of these three objects became the sacred regalia of the emperor. Their exact religious

---

[2]See Michel Revon, "Ancestor-Worship and Cult of the Dead (Japanese)."

I. FORMATION OF JAPANESE RELIGION

significance is problematic but they tell us of two important facts: an increasing continental influence, and a growing consolidation of religion around one center. ?

The Religious Significance of Divine Descent

From about the first to the eighth century A.D. we cross the border from prehistory to early history; in order to describe this period we must rely upon ethnological comparisons and written records, both Chinese and Japanese. For example, the earliest surviving records about Japan are Chinese accounts which suggest both female rulers and female shamans. Moving back in time from the Japanese records we find hints of female shamanism and ruling queens, but they are overshadowed by clans with a man as the political-religious leader. Probably there was a *kami* (god or spirit) for each clan, with rituals performed by the head of the clan. In the light of the northern and southern hypotheses, several inferences have been made about the dual character of the pantheon and religious organization in prehistoric Japan. For example, the southern contribution may have been a horizontal cosmology with the conception that the gods come from afar or across the sea, just as the dead go to this distant land. The northern contribution may have been a vertical cosmology in which the gods are thought to descend from heaven and the dead ascend to heaven. Actually a number of religious elements have been drawn together from diverse areas and periods, such that it is difficult to correlate all these variables. One of the crucial questions is whether the emerging imperial line, which traced its divine descent from the sun, evolved from the earlier Japanese clan system or was an intrusion from the Asian continent. Very old stone circles have been found in Japan which may indicate some kind of solar cult. At any rate, in late Kofun times there appeared a greater sense of political and religious unity. The people came to feel political loyalty and religious respect for the major clan, the budding imperial family which traced its divine descent from the Sun Goddess.

At the end of the prehistoric period, Japanese religion already contained many of the themes which pervade her later history, but as yet they were not organized into set forms. The imperial line was emerging with a nucleus of mythology and agricultural rituals, all of which would be perpetuated mainly within the framework of Shinto. Up to this point neither Shinto nor any other clearly defined religious organization was recognizable. While Shinto increasingly became the main receptacle for the earlier traditions, none of them was transmitted as a pure element, without receiving the influence of Buddhism and Chinese religion. Most of these elements found their way into one or more of the organized religions, while some continued to exist in folk religion outside any organized religion.

SELECTED READINGS
Earhart, H. Byron. *Religion in the Japanese Experience.* See pp. 186–89 for excerpts from Kidder describing prehistoric religion.

Kidder, J. E., Jr. *Japan Before Buddhism.* The best single book on prehistoric Japan, with discussions of the religious implications of the diverse archaeological evidence.

Kitagawa, Joseph M. "Prehistoric Background of Japanese Religion." The best summary of prehistoric religion.

Munro, Neil Gordon. *Ainu Creed and Cult.* A descriptive work based on field work earlier in this century, it includes numerous photographs.

Revon, Michel. "Ancestor-Worship and Cult of the Dead (Japanese)." An early Western discussion of the controversy concerning "ancestor worship" and "nature worship."

Smith, Robert J., and Beardsley, Richard K., ed. *Japanese Culture, Its Development and Characteristics.* Contains articles by leading Japanese scholars on early Japanese culture.

4.
The Formation of Shinto

The Meaning of Shinto in Japanese Religious History

Shinto constitutes a unique contribution of Japan to the history of religions. It arose out of the prehistoric religious practices of the Japanese islands and tended to preserve these practices within modified forms. To a great extent the religious life within Shinto represents a continuity with ancient customs, and therefore enjoys a reputation of long historic association with the Japanese nation. However, it would be a mistake to see Shinto simply as the indigenous and national religion of Japan. A historical tracing of Shinto demonstrates that both its organization and also much of its content owe a great deal to Chinese and Buddhist influence. The blending of Japanese and foreign religious elements into one great national tradition is the distinctive contribution of Shinto.

Shinto forms the next subject for discussion because, historically viewed, it is the channel through which many of the earlier Japanese religious forms were handed down and preserved. However, in discussing Shinto at this point we must realize that we are making a chronological jump past the stimulus provided by the entrance of Buddhism. The time span and complex character of the emergence of Shinto can be appreciated just by looking at the word "Shinto."

For long centuries the religious traditions and practices within the Japanese islands were loosely gathered around separate clans, with no central organization, without even a common name. Gradually the imperial clan and its traditions came to be considered supreme over all the other clans, but still there was no name given to the larger or smaller traditions. Not until Buddhism and advanced Chinese culture entered Japan (about mid-sixth century) was there any need to distinguish the old traditional practices from any contrasting cult. Then, because Buddhism called itself the "way of the Buddha" (Butsudo), the traditional religion set itself apart by the counterpart term Shinto, the "way of the *kami*." The two Chinese characters forming the term Shinto originated in an earlier Chinese term (pronounced *shentao*), but in Japanese it is traditionally understood in the Japanese pronunciation of *kami no michi*, "way of the *kami*." The intention of these words is to indicate the "way of the *Japanese* divinities," even though we recognize various foreign influences upon Shinto as an organized religion.

Mythological Materials and Formative Shinto

A major difficulty in comprehending the formation of Shinto is that as soon as we pass from prehistory into history, Chinese cultural influence is already evident.

In fact, foreign influence is most conspicuous in the written documents because the Japanese had no written language prior to the influx of the Chinese script. The first written records in Japan are the *Kojiki* and *Nihon Shoki* (the latter is known in the West as the *Nihongi*), chronicles compiled on court order and completed in 712 and 720 A.D., respectively. These earliest Japanese documents, as mixtures of cosmology, mythology, and chronicle, are the context in which the earliest forms of Shinto are recorded. Thus, there is good reason to begin an investigation of the formation of Shinto with these two writings.

Although the *Kojiki* and *Nihongi* have often been considered as the watershed of myth from which all later Japanese religion (particularly Shinto) is derived, this general notion is inadequate at two points. In the first place, these scriptures reflect a combination of conscious political and religious motives for unifying Japan at that time. They were compiled by the court elite and did not necessarily constitute the faith of the country at large. In the second place, there is probably no such thing as a foundational myth in the history of Japanese religion. For the Japanese there is neither one sacred myth nor one set of sacred scriptures. Of course, within a primitive tribe there is a common myth which defines the worldview or the emergence of reality. In the so-called higher cultures, such as India, there is a similar function which sacred scriptures like the Vedas have; for the Vedas blend with indigenous Indian motifs to provide the religious base on which later scriptures, commentaries, epics, and even popular dramas are based. However, in Japan there is no common myth or body of religious scripture which pervades the whole religious scene. It is not a question of foreign influence, because almost all myths and scriptures are already synthetic statements; it is simply a fact that the *Kojiki* and *Nihongi* were never that popular.

These reservations concerning the *Kojiki* and *Nihongi* have been made, not to minimize their importance for Japanese religious history, but rather to set them in the proper perspective so that we may better understand them. Now perhaps we can see more clearly the complex character of these ancient writings and their relevance for comprehending the formation of Shinto. For example, the opening passage of the *Nihongi* is a story of creation which is not Japanese, but a borrowing from a Chinese version of creation (in terms of the Chinese bipolarity of *yin* and *yang*—female and male). It appears that the Japanese writers sought prestige for their own traditions by prefacing them with a Chinese form of cosmology. (Throughout Japanese history there has been a mixture of reverence and respect for the cultural tradition of China, to a much greater degree than Europeans glorify their cultural roots in the Greco-Roman tradition.) From this point—the beginning of recorded history in Japan—all things Chinese tended to hold an exalted status in Japanese eyes. Even the notion of possessing a history or tradition and recording it in written form seems to have been borrowed from China. It is important to recognize that these first Japanese books begin with a Chinese note, and that Chinese elements are sprinkled throughout.

The Chinese cosmological element merely sets the stage for introducing the unorganized Japanese traditions. The Chinese contribution is the notion that the

I. FORMATION OF JAPANESE RELIGION

cosmos emerged out of "a chaotic mass like an egg," which then separated into heaven (male) and earth (female). This preface serves as a general explanation for the origin of the world and all the divinities. The first two chapters of these writings, entitled "The Age of the Gods," give a patchwork picture of various traditions concerning the generations of gods and founding of the Japanese islands. In this mythical period seven generations of divinities or *kami* culminated in the marriage of Izanagi (a male *kami*) and Izanami (a female *kami*). They brought about the appearance of the Japanese islands by thrusting the "jewel-spear of Heaven" from the bridge of heaven into the briny waters below. Then they descended to the land which had appeared, and produced other *kami* as well as other features of the universe.

One major theme of the mythology is the descent of the so-called Sun Goddess Amaterasu from this couple, because from Amaterasu comes the imperial line of Japan. Actually, this is only one of a number of themes or cycles which have been blended together into a combination mythology and chronology. In general the other themes have been subordinated to the tradition of an imperial line which descended from the Sun Goddess Amaterasu. One purpose of the two chapters called "The Age of the Gods" is to justify the divine origin of the emperors and empresses whose reigns are recorded in the remainder of the book. As a matter of fact, these chronologies were written down on command of the imperial court. According to one tradition, a person who had memorized all the ancient traditions and genealogies recited these for transcribers (who wrote them down by using Chinese characters). Nevertheless, the records both in their intention and content favor the traditions surrounding the imperial line.

We noted earlier that in ancient Japan there were many clans independent of each other in their religious and political leadership. Probably the imperial line represents the clan (*uji*) which became dominant over the other clans, subsequently unifying the country both politically and religiously. To unify the religion in pre-Buddhist times apparently meant to orient all the competing traditions around the tradition of the ruling clan. After the entrance of Buddhism and advanced Chinese culture, this composite tradition was spiced with Chinese elements for prestige, and written down for the first time.

The *Kojiki* and *Nihongi* are very important in understanding Japanese religion and the formation of Shinto. These works illustrate two all-important religious notions: first, the divine (or semi-divine) descent of Japan and her people, and, second, the proliferation of *kami* intimately related to the land and her people. For example, even in these early records we can recognize the characteristic Japanese love of nature as a combination of religious and aesthetic emotion. These themes are not limited to the *Kojiki* and *Nihongi*; rather, they persisted in the life of the people from prehistoric times onward. "Shinto" is the name applied to the organized religion which attempted to unify and perpetuate these and similar themes.

In this light, it is much easier to understand how, traditionally speaking, a Japanese person could not divorce himself from Shinto. Until recent times Shinto has tended to define the weight of his cultural and religious heritage. On both the local and national plane Shinto hallows his homeland and his people, as well as the nexus of the religious, political, and natural order. Given this situation, we can understand why Shinto scholars proudly emphasize that Shinto is a natural expression of Japanese life, rather than the product of a definite set of doctrines or a conscious conversion. Also, we can realize why there has always been a close association of religious devotion, patriotism, and reverential respect for the emperor. Indeed, the three imperial regalia (sword, mirror, and jewel) were sacred from prehistoric times, as the archaeological evidence proves.

Other early Japanese writings are helpful for understanding the religious context out of which Shinto was formed. The *Manyoshu* is a famous anthology of poetry which blends lyric and religious themes. The *Kogoshui* is a valuable document recording a rivalry between several priestly families. Even as early as the seventh and eighth centuries A.D. there were in existence distinct theological and ritual factions.

Organized Shinto: Priests and Rituals in Shinto Shrines

We have seen that the religio-political combination was present even in the early Japanese clans, and the early government of eighth century Japan continued this tendency by establishing a powerful department of religion as a part of the state's administration. As Sir George Sansom described the department of religion:

> It was concerned with the performance of the great religious ceremonies (such as the rites of enthronement and national purification, and the festivals of the first-fruits and harvest thanksgiving), the upkeep of shrines, the discipline of shrine wardens, and the recording and observance of oracles and divinations. It presided over the worship of the national divinities, and had nothing to do with Buddhism.[1]

We are not surprised to find religion and the priesthood as an arm of the government, because it is only natural for the emperor (as the divine ruler) to be responsible for the ritual as well as the administrative propriety of the realm. In many ancient traditions, the perpetuation of the ritual order was necessary for maintaining the whole cosmic order. However, it is important to note the contents of this ritual.

From Yayoi times to the present, Japanese religion, especially Shinto ceremonies, have been linked with every phase of growing rice. Although rice-planting occasions a festival, this and other phases are overshadowed by the climax of the rice harvest, at which time the new rice is offered up. Even the enthronement ceremony for a new emperor was patterned after the annual thanksgiving

---

[1]Sir George Sansom, *A History of Japan*, Vol. I, p. 68. For a detailed treatment of the department of religion established in 702 A.D., see Sir George Sansom, "Early Japanese Law and Administration."

harvest ceremony. Other important annual ceremonies are the public purifications which take place at the mid-point and the end of the year.

The ritual prayers (*norito*) for the public ceremonies are recorded in the codes called the *Engishiki*. The *Engishiki*, or Codes of the Engi Era, were not written down until 927, but they contain materials which predate this era. In particular the *norito* or liturgies presented in Shinto ceremonies, recorded in the *Engishiki*, are extremely valuable for understanding early Shinto. (See the Selected Readings for translations of *norito*.) The priest who read the *norito* served as an intermediary between men and the *kami*. Usually the priest "called down" the *kami* at the beginning of the ceremony and "sent them away" at the close of the ceremony. Sometimes this was acted out by opening and closing the doors to the inner sanctum (*shinden* or "*kami* hall") housing the sacred object (*shintai* or "*kami* body"), which symbolized the presence of the enshrined *kami*.

The emphasis on purification can be found at a contemporary Shinto shrine (*jinja*). (In English usage the word "shrine" is the general term for the Shinto building—*jinja* or *miya*; the word "temple" is the general term for the Buddhist building—*tera* or *-ji*.) Normally one passes through a sacred arch (*torii*) which helps define the sacred precincts of the shrine, and a devout believer will wash his hands and rinse his mouth to purify himself. The present shrine buildings, of course, betray Buddhist and Chinese architectural influence, but some shrines are still built according to the ancient models. These shrines are built on poles above the ground, with a thatched roof. Such shrines can be seen even today at Ise, one of the Shinto strongholds which consciously attempted to reject Buddhist influence. (At Ise the Sun Goddess Amaterasu is enshrined.) This ancient shrine architecture seems to have affinities with architecture to the south of Japan; as Shinto scholars like to point out, its natural beauty is accentuated by the use of wood and thatch, left bare of decorations.

One theory concerning ancient Japanese religion is that originally there were no shrine buildings; rather, a shrine was simply a sacred precinct set apart in a certain area, or around a sacred object such as a tree or a stone. These sacred precincts often were the sites where the ancestral spirits dwelled. This is a valuable insight for linking ancestor worship with Japanese notions of *kami* and festivals. Only later did there come to appear the twofold Shinto architecture, with a worship hall (*haiden*) in front and a smaller *kami* hall in back. The worship hall is where the priests (and sometimes the people) directed prayers toward the *kami* hall, where the presence of the enshrined *kami* was symbolized by a sacred object such as a mirror or sword. As Shinto became organized in medieval times, every local shrine was considered to enshrine a specific *kami* named in the *Kojiki*.

Religious activities at the Shinto shrine took place in terms of the rhythm of the religious year and an individual's lifespan. Of course, the complicated religious calendar of organized Shinto was the result of borrowing the Chinese calendar system. Nevertheless, even the earlier Japanese religious tradition seems to have observed the rhythm of the year, with spring festivals and fall festivals to mark the planting and harvesting of rice. The spring and fall festivals are still important celebrations in most city shrines. Of great importance, too, were the purification ceremonies at mid-year and New Year's, to wash away the physical and spiritual "pollutions" or "defilements" of the previous half year.[2]

Five traditional festivals (also revealing Chinese influence) which have come to be celebrated throughout Japan are as follows: first day of the first month, New Year's festival; third day of the third month, the girls' festival (or dolls' festival); fifth day of the fifth month, boys' festival; seventh day of the seventh month, star festival; ninth day of the ninth month, chrysanthemum festival. Although this system of five festivals is a complex mixture of Chinese and Japanese elements, they have become inseparable from Japanese home and village life.[3]

Religious activities at the shrine also revolved around the events in an individual life. Traditionally, the newborn child was dedicated at a shrine on his first trip out of the house. At other specific ages a child visited the shrines. Usually there were special youth groups who helped carry out the processions of festivals. In more recent times it has become the custom to be married within the shrine. But a visit to the shrine has always been appropriate in any time of crisis. For example, a soldier going off to war would pray for safekeeping at his local (guardian) shrine where he had been carried as a baby. All such visits to shrines brought the person into contact with the *kami*, the sacred power which sustains human life.

The preceding discussion of the history and nature of Shinto shows how native and foreign elements were blended together into one great national tradition. At the same time the discussion shows that it is a mistake to see Shinto simply as the indigenous and national religion of Japan by falsely contrasting all other traditions as foreign. Nevertheless, many secondary Western interpretations of Shinto perpetuate these misleading notions. Misconceptions arose partly because Western scholars tried too hard to compartmentalize Shinto and Buddhism into separate religions. Also, the emphatically national character of Shinto was overexaggerated by Western scholars who studied Shinto during its nationalistic phase from about 1867 to 1945.[4] Many of the Western materials on Shinto, written during this emotional period leading up to World War II, are less valuable because of their impassioned protest against the national religion of Shinto. It is now time for a re-evaluation of Shinto in more balanced terms. Our treatment of Shinto within this book has nothing to do with arguments for or against a

---

[2]For a brief discussion of early Shinto in terms of purification from pollution, see Geoffrey Bownas, "Shinto."

[3]For the five sacred festivals see U. A. Casal, *The Five Sacred Festivals of Ancient Japan.*

[4]Daniel C. Holtom in his *The National Faith of Japan. A Study of Modern Shinto* described Shinto nationalism in the questionable terms of "tribal religion." See the more balanced discussion of this problem in Ryusaku Tsunoda, *et al., Sources of Japanese Tradition,* Chapter 2.

national religion; rather we simply want to place Shinto within the historical context of Japanese religion.

A brief summary of the formative period of Shinto will help us focus on the significant developments. Of greatest importance is the fact that shortly after Buddhism's appearance from China, Shinto arose and assumed its basic shape. Shinto did not create completely new forms, but organized the pre-existing heritage into a distinctive tradition. This distinctive tradition included a mythology, pantheon, priesthood, liturgies, and shrines. In the *Engishiki*, an official writing of the tenth century, is recorded a system of over 6,000 shrines named in connection with annual offerings from the court. Shinto organized this tradition in reaction to, and partly in imitation of, the Buddhist and Chinese importations. Throughout Japanese history Shinto has manifested a tension between the aim of preserving Japanese traditions and the aim of adopting foreign traditions. Next we will discuss the imported traditions; in Part II we will return to the problem of how Shinto adopted these imported traditions.

SELECTED READINGS

Aston, W.G., trans. *Nihongi. Chronicles of Japan from the Earliest Times to* A.D. *697.* Contains practices and mythology that entered Shinto.

Bock, Felicia Gressitt, trans. *Engi-Shiki: Procedures of the Engi Era, Books I-V.* A translation of eighth century government regulations concerning Shinto shrines, their administration, and rituals; includes introductory chapters on early Shinto.

————, trans. *Engi-Shiki: Procedures of the Engi Era, Books VI-X.* Continuation of the preceding work.

Chamberlain, Basil Hall, trans. "*Kojiki*, or Records of Ancient Matters." The oldest written record in Japan, contains practices and mythology that entered Shinto.

Earhart, H. Byron. *Religion in the Japanese Experience.* See Part Two for selected documents on Shinto, including excerpts from Holtom and the *Kojiki;* see also pp. 128–30 for excerpts from the *Manyoshu,* and pp. 162–66 for the translation of a *norito.*

Holtom, Daniel C. *The National Faith of Japan. A Study in Modern Shinto.* A prewar study of Shinto, still valuable for its historical information.

Kato, Genchi, and Hoshino, Hikoshiro, trans. *Kogoshui. Gleanings from Ancient Stories.* Written about 807 A.D., it records a rivalry between several Shinto priestly families.

The Manyoshu. The earliest recorded Japanese poetry, it mirrors early religious attitudes.

Mizoguchi, Komazo. "Orientation in the Study of Shintoism." A prewar attempt to establish a historical-scientific study of Shinto.

Phillipi, Donald L., trans. *Kojiki.* A recent translation emphasizing linguistic accuracy.

————, trans. *Norito. A New Translation of the Ancient Japanese Ritual Prayers.* The most recent English translation of the *norito,* with brief notes.

Satow, Sir Ernest, and Florenz, Karl. "Ancient Japanese Rituals." An older translation of the *norito,* with illustrations and commentary on their religious significance.

Ueda, Kenji. "Shinto," in *Japanese Religion,* edited by Ichiro Hori, pp. 29–45. A concise overview of the aspects and dynamics of Shinto.

5.
Early Japanese Buddhism: Indian Influence with Chinese Coloration

The Introduction of Buddhism as a Foreign Religion

By the time Buddhism reached Japanese shores it had already been transformed within India as well as in the passage across the Asian continent. In this book we can treat only the place of Buddhism within Japanese religious history. On the one hand, Buddhism made a tremendous contribution to the religious scene in Japan; on the other hand, Buddhism was transformed by weight of the Japanese tradition. The twofold result is that while Japan became a Buddhist nation, Buddhism became a Japanese religion. In the initial or formative period it was the Buddhist impact upon Japanese culture and religion that was conspicuous. In the second or developmental period the Japanese transformation of Buddhism became more conspicuous.

Within Buddhist history there have come to be two major divisions along the lines of geography, doctrine, and practice. To the south of India, in countries such as Ceylon and Burma, there continued the tradition of monastic Buddhism which emphasized strict adherence to monastic rules or discipline, preservation of the scriptures of the Buddha, and doctrines which made salvation a long and difficult road for laymen. This division is often called Southern Buddhism or Theravada (School of the Elders, or Monks). To the north of India and spreading across China to Japan, there continued the form of Buddhism which placed less importance on monastic discipline and greater importance on later scriptures (such as the Lotus Sutra), aspiration to the status of a Buddha, and rebirth in a heavenly paradise. Especially because this Northern Buddhism insisted on the easy path to salvation for all people, it called itself Mahayana (the Large or Great Way) and gave Southern Buddhism the name Hinayana (the Small or Inferior Way). Although there are many similarities between these two divisions of Buddhism, and although the traditions of Southern Buddhism were brought to China and Japan, it was the Mahayana form of Buddhism which made the decisive impact in the Far East.

Buddhism entered Japan by way of Korea in the mid-sixth century. (Most authorities prefer the formal date of 552 A.D. or 538 A.D., even though Buddhist influence may have been present earlier.) The *Nihongi* records the first Japanese reference to Buddhism, when one of the Korean kings sent tribute to the Japanese emperor, including an image of Buddha and Chinese translations of Buddhist scriptures. The Korean king praised Buddhism as the religion of distant India whose doctrine surpasses even the understanding of the Chinese, and whose value is without limit. The introduction of Buddhism into Japan automatically provoked a conflict with the pre-existing religious tradition. We have indicated in the previous chapter that this conflict was what stimulated the adoption of the name "Shinto" and the formal organization of the pre-existing tradition. However, the argument between budding Shinto and Buddhism was not carried on in terms of doctrine. Instead, the crucial question was whether or not to worship the statue of Buddha. (Buddhist art has exerted an amazing influence on Japanese religion and culture—the most conspicuous feature of the Buddhist temple is the presence of numerous statues of Buddhist divinities.) Naturally, the Korean descendants favored the adoption of Buddha-worship, whereas the Japanese families, priests of budding Shinto, maintained a firm opposition. The cult of Buddha underwent some sudden reversals, as in the case when a pestilence was attributed to the wrath of the national gods because the people were worshiping foreign deities. Eventually Buddhism became accepted as one of the religions of the realm, being elevated from a private cult celebrated in private homes to a state religion partly responsible for the welfare of the country.

Buddhism's Impact on the Court and the State

The story of early Buddhism in Japan is Buddhism's acceptance by the clan leaders, then by the imperial court, and finally by the state. Later diplomatic missions from Korea brought more Buddhist images and scriptures, but most important was the arrival of Buddhist priests. At this time the Japanese were just learning to manage the Chinese writing system, so it took a specially trained Buddhist priest to read and expound the Chinese translations of Buddhist scriptures. Also, the Buddhist priests began to serve the religious needs of the court and state. In the private sphere Buddhism came to be appropriated for every imaginable occasion, one of the most important of which was the Buddhist memorial service. Already by the first years of the eighth century a Buddhist priest and an empress set the Japanese precedent of having their bodies cremated, a Buddhist innovation. Memorial services were practiced by Buddhist priests as early as 616, when a Shinto shrine oracle "declared that Buddhist priests were the proper persons to perform funeral rites."[1] Buddhist priests recited scriptures for the repose of souls, accepted ashes of the dead for safekeeping in their temples, and performed memorial services at regular intervals. Wooden memorial tablets *(ihai)* were enshirined in the family Buddhist altar *(butsudan),* and often cemeteries with memorial gravestones grew up around Buddhist temples.[2] In addition

---

[1]Sir Charles Eliot, *Japanese Buddhism,* p. 203.

[2]For funeral rites, see Arthur Hyde Lay, "Japanese Funeral Rites." An excerpt from this work is included in H. Byron Earhart, *Religion in the Japanese Experience,* pp. 61–64.

to memorial services, members of the court had scriptures read for such purposes as relieving sickness and easing childbirth. In this case and throughout Japanese history, Buddhism's influence was due not only to the profundity of its doctrine, but also to its great appeal on the level of art, ritual, and magic. As a matter of fact, Buddhist magical formulas were brought to Japan together with formal scriptures, and even the Buddha was worshiped as a *kami.* Already in this early period Buddhism presented a religious pattern quite similar to Shinto, with its appeal to divine powers for immediate human needs. Shinto had its shrines, *kami,* ritual prayers *(norito),* and priests. Buddhism likewise had its temples, Buddhas or Buddhist divinities, scriptures and rites, and priests. Buddhism had its own way of bringing men to religious fulfillment or sacred power, conceived in Buddhist terms.

At the same time that Buddhism was being accepted by the court in the private sphere, it was being accepted by the state in the public sphere. We can even say that Buddhism played a major role in shaping the Japanese state, so great was its influence. It is worth noting the contrast between the acceptance of Buddhism in China and in Japan. China possessed a rich tradition of literature, philosophy, religion, and government, such that Buddhism had to fight an uphill battle to be accepted. By contrast, Japan had no literature and philosophy to speak of, and her religion and government were only loosely formed. It is no wonder, then, that Buddhism and Chinese culture together exerted such a great influence on Japanese culture and religion. The budding Japanese attempts to unify and centralize their country were greatly aided by the stimulus and even some of the models of highly organized Chinese culture. The Buddhist priests in early Japan possessed two highly valued treasures: the religious heritage of Indian Buddhism in the garb of Chinese language and custom, and the cultural heritage of China which included the models for a well-ordered kingdom. Buddhist priests also brought to Japan many technical skills associated with Buddhism, such as carpentry and architecture. For centuries to come priests played a major role in the importation and implementation of Chinese models of government. A number of Buddhist priests, who went from Japan to China on court order, combined commercial, religious, and governmental functions.

Not only Buddhist priests, but also the emperors themselves were partly responsible for the importance of this religion in state affairs. Of the sixth-century Emperor Yomei, it is said that he "believed in the Law of the Buddha and reverenced the Way of the Gods" (Shinto).[3] (Plurality of religions is the rule rather than the exception in Japanese history.) Prince Shotoku (573–621), second son of Emperor Yomei, is considered to be the actual founder of Japanese Buddhism. He had built at Nara a large temple complex, Horyu-ji, housing many fine examples of Buddhist art. According to tradition, Prince Shotoku saw in Buddhism both a profound philosophy of life and a sound foundation for the state. He demonstrated his scholarship and devotion by writing several commentaries

---

[3] *Nihongi. Chronicles of Japan from the Earliest Times to* A.D. *697,* Vol. II, p. 106.

on difficult Buddhist scriptures; furthermore he declared Buddhism to be one of the pillars of the state (together with Confucianism) in his famous set of principles or "Constitution" of seventeen articles.[4] This marked the first major recognition of Buddhism's profound message and the outstanding precedent of Buddhism as the rationale for the state. From this point on, until about the nineteenth century, Buddhism tended to overshadow Shinto.

We must remember that this was a formative period for Japanese history, during which time the Japanese tried to utilize Chinese models to organize Japanese society. Buddhism was one element included within this program of organization, but also was an active force in determining how the organizing activity took place. For example, as early as 624 A.D. Empress Suiko regulated the Buddhist priesthood, establishing the supervision of monks and nuns. The Taiho code of 702 included several sections dealing with religious administration, including the organization of the Shinto bureau and the bureau of *Onmyo* (the Japanese version of the Chinese bureau of *yin* and *yang*). There was a special section of the code dealing with the regulation of monks and nuns.[5] Buddhism had become so flourishing that the state had to step in to curb excesses and maintain religious uniformity. However, if the state tended to control Buddhism, Buddhism in turn tended to unify and support the state.

Buddhism as a State Religion

During the Nara period (710–784, named after the capital city of Nara), Buddhism became a state religion, for all practical purposes. Emperor Shomu (reigned 724–749), one of the most devout emperors, contributed greatly to Buddhism's national status. The greatest symbol of the unifying power of Buddhism was a central cathedral built at Nara in 728, on the order of Emperor Shomu. This was the famous temple called Todai-ji (Todai temple), still a popular tourist attraction due to the large Buddha statue enshrined therein. There were six formal schools of Buddhism in the Nara period, and technically Todai-ji was the headquarters of one of these schools, the Kegon school. However, in actuality Todai-ji was a central cathedral within the capital which protected the emperor and the realm, as well as unifying Buddhism throughout the provinces.

In 741 Emperor Shomu ordered "provincial temples" *(kokubunji)* to be built in every province. Ideally every province was supposed to build both a monastery and a nunnery, the monks and nuns of which would recite Buddhist scriptures; this served as a protection and blessing for the whole countryside. In Buddhism the copying and reciting of scriptures—even thumbing through scriptures, or chanting short phrases—has always been considered as enabling the person to

---

[4]Ibid., Vol. II, pp. 128–33 for the text of this "Constitution." An excerpt of this work is included in H. Byron Earhart, *Religion in the Japanese Experience,* pp. 202–3.

[5]See Sir George Sansom, "Early Japanese Law and Administration," Part II, pp. 127–34 for a translation of "The Law Concerning Monks and Nuns."

accumulate ethical merit or magical power. The peculiarity in this case is that the nation at large was the recipient of these benefits. The main temple which controlled the provincial temples was the famous Todai-ji of Nara. Not only was Todai-ji a geographical and administrative center, but also served as a religious focus. A large Buddhist statue (of the Sun Buddha Lochana) was erected within Todai-ji, the funds for which are said to have been raised by popular subscription. It is worth noting that the country was united symbolically in the erection of this large statue through popular donations. One might say that the people were able to find an even greater sense of religious and national unity in Buddhism than in Shinto, for at that time the people were not directly related to the emperor. Moreover, the Shinto rituals involving the imperial family, although national in significance, allowed little possibility for any sense of participation by the common people.

Most scholars feel that by this time Buddhism already overshadowed Shinto; in fact Shinto tended to borrow on the glory of Buddhism. The two traditions already had begun interacting with each other, as two interesting developments at Todai-ji illustrate. Worship of the large Buddhist statue was facilitated by invoking the presence of a divinity called Hachiman, who became a tutelary deity of Todai-ji. The origin of Hachiman may be Chinese or Buddhist or both, but already by this time Hachiman was considered a Shinto deity or *kami*. However, Hachiman was also called *bosatsu*. *Bosatsu* is the Japanese equivalent of the Buddhist term *bodhisattva* (in Sanskrit), which means here a Buddhist divinity. The word *bodhisattva* means a being "destined for enlightenment," and can even refer to a living person or "saint" who is inferior only to the Buddha himself. Hachiman enjoyed a rich history in later Japan, but always incorporated both Shinto and Buddhist features. Also we may note that Lochana, the large Buddhist statue in Todai-ji, was a form of the so-called Sun Buddha (Dainichi or Birushana in Japanese, Vairocana in Sanskrit). According to one tradition, messengers had to be sent to Ise to gain the approval of the Sun Goddess Amaterasu of Shinto for the erection of this statue. The answer of the oracle seemed to indicate that the Sun Buddha was indeed identical to the Sun Goddess. The tradition of this oracle may not date back to the eighth century, but in later times the two were closely associated, just as so many Buddhist divinities and Shinto *kami* came to be considered as counterparts. Several centuries later, in all Japan we find popular conceptions which blended together a local spirit or *kami*, a formal member of the Shinto pantheon, and a Buddhist divinity—into one and the same object of worship.

Our overall impression of Buddhism up through the Nara period (eighth century) is that it had become firmly entrenched in the hearts of the nobility and the bureaucracy of the state. On the other hand, the popular acceptance of Buddhism was not nearly so widespread. Even the attempt to propagate Buddhism to the masses was carried out by only a few devoted priests. Gyogi, the most famous of them, not only preached to the people, but also promoted the popularity of Buddhism through charitable projects such as founding hospitals.

He was even granted the posthumous title of *bosatsu,* equivalent to saint. The inclusion of "The Law Concerning Monks and Nuns" in the Taiho code of 702 was an admission that the masses were beginning to accept Buddhism, but it also reflected the state effort to control the activities of clerics in the spread of Buddhism. We might say that Buddhism already was considered a state religion of Japan, and later, with increasing popularity, became a national religion of Japan. Buddhism tended to dominate the whole religious scene, but actually paralleled Shinto rather than superseded it.

The Six Philosophical Schools of Nara Buddhism

The general picture of Nara Buddhism suggests a religion of the aristocracy and monks, largely confined to the court and monasteries. During this period numerous sumptuous temples were founded, many of which can be seen at Nara today. Although these wooden structures have been frequently damaged by fires, they are accurately rebuilt and house some of the oldest treasures of Japan, including some items from ancient China and beyond. In their flourishing period these large temples were overflowing with scholar monks, who frequently catered to the religious needs of the court and state, but were primarily committed to scholarship on Buddhist scriptures and doctrines. In the Nara period the state recognized six divisions within Buddhism, which were more of the nature of philosophical schools than full-fledged religious sects. In brief, these schools transmitted the philosophical heritage of Indian Buddhism in the vessels of Chinese translations, but there was no original Japanese contribution at this point. Although these schools are of the greatest importance for tracing Buddhist philosophy from India to Japan, they are of lesser consequence for understanding Japanese religion. Therefore, we touch on them but briefly in order to illustrate the diversity of the religious heritage in Japan.

The six schools and their traditional dates of entry into Japan are: Jojitsu (625), Sanron (625), Hosso (654), Kusha (658), Kegon (736), Ritsu (738). Each school was oriented around one (or several) of the classic Buddhist scriptures (in Chinese translation), expounding and defining the viewpoint of their distinctive scripture. According to one Japanese scholar, the Jojitsu and Kusha schools were of minor importance since they did not "have a significant separate existence."[6] The Sanron school continued one of the most glorious philosophical streams of Buddhism, including the Madhyamika philosophy of Nagarjuna. The Hosso schools prepetuated the "consciousness-only" philosophy which played a great role in Chinese Buddhism. The Kegon school has been of great intellectual influence on Japanese Buddhism, as its affiliation with Todai-ji might suggest. The Ritsu school concerned itself with Buddhism's monastic discipline. ("Discipline"

---

[6]Shinsho Hanayama, "Buddhism in Japan," p. 315. A brief treatment of the six schools will be found in any general work such as Hanayama or Sir Charles Eliot, *Japanese Buddhism.*

is *Vinaya* in Sanskrit, Ritsu in Japanese.) The Ritsu school was important for establishing the rules and actual altars for ordination (one of which was established before the great Buddha at Todai-ji), but in general Japanese Buddhism has not conformed to all the Indian prescriptions of discipline. These philosophical schools were not mutually exclusive in Japan even in the beginning, since priests often studied the doctrines of several schools. A number of the famous old temples, especially those at Nara, are still counted as belonging to one of the six schools, but for the most part the schools live on today as indirect intellectual influences within the later sects of Japanese Buddhism. The schools, although never popular in scope, represent the philosophical resource for Japanese Buddhism and much Japanese thought.

If Nara Buddhism became famous for its profound philosophy and glorious temples, it became infamous for its increasing decadence and corruption. Japan is no exception to the rule that money and power tend to corrupt. The Nara temples grew in prestige and wealth by attracting bequests from the nobility and favoritism from the state. In turn, the prestige and wealth of the temples attracted politically ambitious men to the priesthood. In a short time these temples had become so wealthy and their priests so powerful that their interference in the politics of the capital could not be tolerated. This condition seems to have been a primary factor in moving the capital from Nara to Kyoto in the transitional period from 784 to 794. (Before the Nara period it was the normal custom to move the capital at the death of every emperor, supposedly on the belief that the emperor's death defiled the capital.) This move freed the court from the intrigues of the Nara temples which were left behind in the former capital; the move also signalled the need for a religious renewal, a need which was met in the next period by the new Buddhist sects of Tendai and Shingon.

Selected Readings

de Visser, Marinus Willem. *Ancient Buddhism in Japan.* A technical, detailed account of scriptures and ceremonies in early Japanese Buddhism.

Earhart, H. Byron. *Religion in the Japanese Experience.* See Part Three for selected documents on Japanese Buddhism, including excerpts from Lay.

Eliot, Sir Charles. *Japanese Buddhism.* A standard handbook, emphasizing continuity with Indian and Chinese Buddhism.

Hanayama, Shinsho, *et al.* "Buddhism in Japan." A short treatment by leading Japanese scholars.

———. "Orientation in the Study of Japanese Buddhism." Treats the problems of approaching the subject, and emphasizes the uniquely *Japanese* character of Japanese Buddhism.

Kitagawa, Joseph M. "The Buddhist Transformation in Japan." Shows how Buddhism was transformed in Japan, becoming related to both national polity and folk piety.

Kiyota, Minoru. "Presuppositions to the Understanding of Japanese Buddhist Thought." A technical analysis of Japanese Buddhism in relation to Mahayana philosophy. (See also his forthcoming book on Japanese Buddhism.)

Lay, Arthur Hyde. "Japanese Funeral Rites." A general survey, including both Buddhist and Shinto practices.

Saunders, E. Dale. *Buddhism in Japan. With an Outline of Its Origins in India.* A recent survey emphasizing the significance of esoteric Buddhism.

Tamaru, Noriyoshi. "Buddhism," in *Japanese Religion,* edited by Ichiro Hori, pp. 47–69. A concise overview of the origin and historical development of Japanese Buddhism.

6.
Confucianism and Religious Taoism in Japan: Chinese Importations

Confucianism: Explicit Chinese Influence on State and Society

Confucianism and religious Taoism were originally religious traditions of China. Their importation into Japan was an important, lasting influence within Japanese religious history. In their Chinese origin Confucianism and religious Taoism were separate traditions, but even before entering Japan they had begun to blend with each other. It is not known exactly when and how they entered Japan, but it most likely occurred about the time of Buddhism's entry in the sixth century together with the flood of Chinese culture.

Neither Confucianism nor religious Taoism constitutes a separate religion in Japanese history. Nevertheless, both traditions made an important contribution to the life of the people and to the other religious traditions. Confucianism played an explicit role in the religious and ethical foundation of the government and also influenced general conceptions of social relations. Religious Taoism started out as a government bureau and ended up as an implicit but pervasive influence on popular beliefs.

It is not surprising that Confucianism would have such great impact in early Japan, for Confucianism was the guiding light of the entering Chinese culture which was in the highest esteem. The early attempt to organize the Japanese nation along Chinese lines is recorded in the first great era or name-period of Japanese history, the Taika ("Great Change") period of 645–710. We have to remember that Confucianism by this time was far removed from the person Confucius, having developed into a political philosophy which incorporated various elements and tended to dominate Chinese civilization. In general, Confucianism as a political philosophy was explicitly and implicitly accepted by the Japanese in borrowing Chinese models of government. The great Prince Shotoku is credited with recognizing the true principles of Confucianism in his "Constitution" of seventeen articles. Buddhist influence is found in this document, but the main rationale behind it is Confucian political and ethical thought. Indeed, the opening statement of the first clause reads: "Harmony is to be valued," a direct borrowing from the *Analects* of Confucius. The Japanese, still trying to unify their country effectively, found a powerful rationale in the Confucian notion of social harmony: the ruler rules justly, the ministers administer honestly, and most important, the people are united in their loyalty to the emperor. Shotoku's Constitution, as well as the other adaptations of Chinese bureaucracies and codes, all supported the Japanese emperor as a true Son of Heaven—the Chinese notion of a heavenly ordained ruler. This idea supported the theory of the divine descent of the Japanese emperor as much as, or more than, the native tradition of his descent from the Sun Goddess Amaterasu. (However, the two countries differed on one important point. In China it was Heaven who appointed the ruler by bestowing a "heavenly mandate"; Heaven could withdraw the heavenly mandate from a corrupt dynasty in order to give it to a new dynasty. In Japan the imperial line was permanently founded as the continuation of the heavenly gods and could never be broken.)

Even though Confucianism was not a separate religion, it constituted an integral factor in the complex of the Japanese tradition. The Confucian character was stamped on the structure of the government and official codes (such as the Taiho Code of 702 A.D.). Even the Confucian precedent of civil service examinations was followed. At the same time, Confucianism was instilled in the minds of the learned class by means of an educational system which emphasized study of the Chinese Classics. Confucianism became more directly related to government policy when it reentered Japanese history as Neo-Confucianism about the fifteenth and sixteenth centuries. This development will be touched on later.

Confucianism has also played a crucial role in the formation of social attitudes and the reinforcement of social institutions. The Confucianism transmitted to Japan emphasized a hierarchically arranged class society and compliance to this order. The "harmony" that the Confucian rationale praised was the peaceful cooperation between benevolent rulers and obedient people. According to the Confucian model, just as earth is subordinate to heaven, so the ruled are subordinate to the ruler. There is a cosmic order which sets the pattern for the social order. Increasingly Confucianism provided the main ethical model for social action, and the model was interpreted as prescribing loyalty to specific social groups.

One of the most important social virtues adopted from Confucianism was filial piety. In this case a borrowed ethical model was used to reinforce and expand preexisting Japanese social institutions such as the family. The Japanese people had revered the dead from prehistoric times, and openly accepted the Confucian notion of filial piety to idealize and elaborate the practice. (At the same time they utilized Buddhist memorial rites to sanctify this practice.) Clans had been important before the arrival of Confucianism, but later all social groups tended to incorporate the rationale of filial piety. Families, of course, drew much of their strength from the fact that they were economic units in such activities as farming, but they came to *understand* their unity through Confucian notions. Later the warrior came to see his relationship to his lord as a combination of duty and privilege defined by absolute loyalty. One can even see this hierarchical authority in more recent times. For example, even in the past century of rapid modernization, the government has taken the initiative in telling the people what they must do, and the people usually have complied. Both Prince Shotoku's so-called "Constitution" of the seventh century and Emperor Meiji's Constitution of the late nineteenth century were handed down on the initiative of the ruler. In Anglo-Saxon history there is abundant precedent of the people *demanding* their rights from the monarch, but the Japanese tendency has been for the people to wait for the imperial rescript or the military ruler's command. Especially during her rapid modernization and military campaigns of the past century, there was an explicit identity of a man's filial piety to his father, his absolute loyalty to the emperor, and his supreme sacrifice for his country. Confucianism was not solely responsible for these social attitudes and institutions; rather such facts demonstrate the extent to which Confucianism was adapted to Japanese conditions. Eventually such notions as filial piety became synonomous with being a good child and a good Japanese citizen. Confucian ideas became closely tied to the very process of growing up and becoming a member of society. This can be illustrated roughly by a comparison of recent child-rearing techniques in the West and in Japan. In the West children are encouraged to become independent and "stand on their own two feet"; in Japan children are brought up to be more dependent on and loyal to the family. In this manner the ideals of Confucianism were woven into the fabric of Japanese society.

Taoism: Implicit Chinese Influence on Beliefs and Rituals

Religious Taoism is perhaps even more complex than Confucianism. We can distinguish two types of Taoism in China: the early Taoism of philosophical texts (like the famous *Tao Te Ching*) and the later blending of this philosophy with various popular beliefs and practices. The popular movement, called "religious Taoism," incorporates an amazing array of religious expressions within one system. It borrowed from several earlier cosmological systems, continued the Taoistic quest for long life, worshiped a large pantheon, practiced alchemy, carried out divination and magic, and generally associated itself with things occult.

As Japan borrowed Buddhism and Confucianism from China, it also borrowed religious Taoism. In Japan religious Taoism is known technically as Dokyo, which is the Japanese pronunciation for the Chinese term Tao-chiao. This phrase means literally the "teaching of the Tao or Way," indicating the "Way" of the universe. But in Japanese religious history the term "religious Taoism" is usually understood in the broader sense of including Onmyo-do (the way of *yin-yang*), as well as many popular practices.

Religious Taoism made its way into Japan via several channels. The books of religious Taoism were brought to Japan at an early date. The practices of religious Taoism were adopted at the court, and in the Taiho Code of 702 a bureau of religious Taoism (Onmyo-ryo) was organized. The officials of this bureau studied the books and performed the divinations, astronomical and astrological, and other practices prescribed therein. One of their chief tasks was the regulation of the calendar. In addition, many of the popular divinities and cults of religious Taoism were accepted in early Japan. In a more elusive fashion the love of nature in religious Taoism influenced Japanese arts, especially landscape painting. We cannot trace the complicated histories of these various elements, but a look at some important features of religious Taoism will indicate its significance for understanding Japanese religious history.

The most conspicuous Japanese example of religious Taoism is the governmental bureau Onmyo-ryo which existed as early as 675 and was officially organized by the Taiho Code. Sansom has provided a translation of the original legislation defining the Onmyo-ryo or "Bureau of Divination."[1] Its governmental responsibility was especially to regulate divination, astrology, and the calendar. To understand the Onmyo-ryo we have to understand the complex of Chinese thought on which it was based. The word *onmyo* is simply the Japanese pronunciation for the Chinese term *yin-yang*. The Chinese term *yin-yang* refers to two complementary forces of the universe which must balance each other if there is to be harmony in the universe. *Yin* is the principle of darkness, cold, femininity, even numbers, and other allied characteristics. *Yang* is the principle of brightness, heat, masculinity, odd numbers, and similar characteristics. The interaction of *yin* and *yang* produces matter which consists of five elements: wood, fire, earth, metal, and water. (Originally in China the theory of *yin-yang* and the theory of five elements were unrelated concepts. Before entering Japan the theories became inseparably related in a unified cosmology.) These sets of forces or elements interact, not only in terms of space, but also in terms of time. In short, this system of thought presupposes a living universe composed of opposing or complementary forces. Ideally these forces can be harmonized, as in the harmonious result of a properly conducted orchestra; if the forces get out of balance, the result is disharmony and catastrophe.

The role of the bureau of divination was to make sure the order of government and society conformed to the cosmic order. Unusual natural phenomena were thought to constitute the universe's expression of harmony or disharmony —omens whose significance was interpreted by this bureau. Therefore it was only natural that the bureau of divination should regulate the calendar so that man's time would correspond to cosmic time. The introduction of the Chinese calander was of the greatest importance to Japanese religious history, for it seems that earlier the Japanese had only a seasonal calendar. The Chinese calendar— adopted and modified in folk religion, Shinto, and Buddhism—carried with it the cosmological theories and beliefs of religious Taoism.[2]

Of course, not many people understood all the intricacies of this cosmic scheme. Nevertheless, the system made inroads into every corner of popular beliefs. One way in which religious Taoism filtered down to the masses was

---

[1]See Sir George Sansom, "Early Japanese Law and Administration," Part I, p. 81.

[2]For a general picture of the Japanese calendar, see Ernest Clement, "Calendar (Japanese)."

6. Confucianism and Religious Taoism   *35*

through popular diviners. Gradually the official members of the Onmyo-ryo gave way to popular diviners who served various religious needs. The popular diviners continued to spread the popular beliefs in religious Taoism, further stimulating the widespread demand for diviners. These popular practitioners of religious Taoism merged with the wandering semi-ascetics of "folk Buddhism."

During the Heian period religious Taoism entered Shinto and Buddhism in the guise of formulas, charms, and cosmological theories. Eventually the various divinities of religious Taoism became accepted within both Shinto and Buddhism, almost losing their original Taoistic identity. Many of the most typical Japanese beliefs about lucky days and lucky directions came from religious Taoism. In medieval novels the movements of the characters ever and again were determined by the stars and the "unlucky directions." From the Heian period onward the beliefs of religious Taoism became a dominant factor in everyday life. To be sure, the people at large understood neither the Chinese origin nor the complete system of religious Taoism, but nevertheless it greatly influenced their lives.

The influence of religious Taoism is difficult to assess because it became so thoroughly Japanized. Taoistic festivals, legends, and cults became woven right into the fabric of Japanese life. For example, the Taoist mountain wizards of China (*hsien* in Chinese, *sen* or *sennin* in Japanese) were thought to dwell also in the Japanese mountains. Another example of Taoistic influence is the cult and belief called Koshin. This cult is typical of Japanese village associations organized for worship of specific divinities at regular intervals. In fact, it is so typical, so blended with Shinto and Buddhist elements, that its Taoist origin was completely forgotten by the cult members.

To sum up these two Chinese importations, both Confucianism (later Neo-Confucianism) and religious Taoism were made over into Japanese possessions. However, Confucianism's role is more easily recognized, since it functioned more explicitly as an official philosophy of the learned classes and the state. (Confucianism became so thoroughly Japanized that it was used as a Japanese propaganda tool for governing both Korea and Manchuria up to 1945.) By contrast, Taoism's influence was more indirect or implicit, and more difficult to recognize. Religious Taoism has been singled out for attention here to indicate its widespread impact on Japanese religion.

SELECTED READINGS

de Bary, William Theodore, *et al. Sources of Chinese Tradition.* A convenient sourcebook for the Chinese background of Japanese culture.

Earhart, H. Byron. *Religion in the Japanese Experience.* See Part Four for selected documents on Confucianism, including excerpts from Smith, and Part Five for selected documents on religious Taoism, including excerpts from Saunders.

Frank, Bernard. "Kata-imi et Kata-tagae. Étude sur les Interdits de direction a l'époque Heian." A technical treatment of the influence of religious Taoism upon medieval literature.

Kubo, Noritada. "Introduction of Taoism to Japan." A brief summary of an important Taoist cult by the foremost scholar on the subject.

Miller, Alan L. "Ritsuryo Japan: The State as Liturgical Community." Includes descriptions of the Bureau of Yin and Yang (Onmyo-ryo) in early Japan.
Saunders, E. Dale. "Koshin; An Example of Taoist Ideas in Japan." Analyzes the history of Koshin and its dynamics as a Taoist cult.
Smith, Warren W., Jr. *Confucianism in Modern Japan.* Treats Confucianism's cultural impact in Japan from 1600 through postwar times.
Spae, Joseph John. *Ito Jinsai. A Philosopher, Educator and Sinologist of the Tokugawa Period.* The first chapter is especially helpful for its historical overview of Confucianism in Japan.
Tomikura, Mitsuo. "Confucianism," in *Japanese Religion,* edited by Ichiro Hori, pp. 105–22. A concise overview of the role of Confucianism in Japanese thought and society.
Tsunoda, Ryusaku, *et al. Sources of Japanese Tradition.* See Chapter 4 for the introduction of Chinese thought and institutions into Japan.

7.

Folk Religion: Religiosity Outside Organized Religion

Folk Religion in Japan

In Japan much religious life is practiced informally, without the direct aid of formal religion. Organized religion (Shinto, Buddhism, Taoism, and Confucianism) is much more conspicuous due to its easily identified writings, priests, liturgies, shrines, and temples. Because of the informal character of folk religion, it does not lend itself to simple identification and historical tracing; nevertheless it is extremely important for the religious experience of the people, particularly in the premodern period. We must remember that every literate culture has a "little tradition" as well as a "great tradition."[1] The great tradition within a culture such as Japan's is the written tradition formally recorded and consciously used by such major institutions as the state and organized religion. The little tradition is the unwritten sets of customs handed down orally within such contexts as family, village, and occupations.

In Japan there are at least three aspects of folk religion: 1) indigenous folk religion, 2) popular religion, and 3) local customs. Indigenous folk religion is the sum of all the unorganized forms of ancient Japanese religion. These forms often became overlaid with the structures of organized religion, but they existed prior to the organized tradition, and often these folk practices coexisted with the more formal traditions. One might say that indigenous folk religion "filtered up" into Shinto and Buddhism. An example of indigenous folk religion is the agricultural rituals associated with the growing of rice, especially rice transplanting celebrations, which were never fully incorporated into organized religion.

Popular religion is made up of the popular expressions of organized religion. Although a religion like Buddhism has its own doctrinal, ritual, and ecclesiastical orthodoxy, in the process of its acceptance by the mass of laymen it undergoes considerable reformulation. From a scholarly or ecclesiastical viewpoint, popular Buddhism may diverge from more orthodox formulas, but the thrust of popular religion is to provide direct access to spiritual resources in the language and style of the people. Popular religion generally can be described as the result of organized religion "filtering down" to the people. An example of popular religion is the kind of neighborhood club (ko) which meets once a month to venerate a

---

[1]See Robert Redfield, *Peasant Society and Cultures* (Chicago: The University of Chicago Press, 1956), p. 70.

divinity, usually a Buddhist divinity; formally the custom derives from Buddhism, but it is expressed and handed down by the people themselves in their own homes.

Local customs refer to the peculiar regional and local practices which usually ③ combine features of indigenous folk religion and popular religion. From ancient times there was no standardization of religion, and religious practices were heavily influenced by the dominant legends, customs, and activities of the surrounding region. Even Shinto and Buddhism lack the centralized uniformity found in Roman Catholicism and Protestant denominations, allowing them to develop more peculiarly local practices. This aspect of folk religion is what contributes so much local color to Japanese religion. An example of such a local usage would be the preservation of a mythical tale or legend associated only with the region (such as the visit of a specific *kami* to the area in ancient times). This tale may be memorialized in a local shrine or temple, and often is dramatized in an annual village festival. Sometimes the occasion for a local custom is a universal religious event, such as the Buddhist festival of the dead, *bon*, but there are local variations on the manner of celebration, such as special village gatherings and specially prepared foods.

These three aspects of folk religion cannot be sharply separated from one another, for they form the living fabric of the everyday practice of religion in traditional Japan. For example, the folk tale can be found in all three aspects as a kind of informal scripture that unifies and preserves religion within the lives of the people. It would also be impossible to completely separate these folk religious elements from organized religion, since there is a great deal of mutual influence between the folk and organized traditions. Considered as a whole, folk religion may be understood as one dimension, the "little tradition" of Japanese religious life. In premodern times this kind of folk religion was the main channel of expression for the religious beliefs and practices of the Japanese laymen, particularly within the agricultural setting of the countryside and farm villages. However, in more recent times folk religious beliefs and activities have become severely abbreviated, due to the expansion of cities and commerce in the late medieval period, and due to the increasing dominance of an urban-industrial way of life after 1868. It is more difficult to trace the historical development of folk religion (as can be done with organized religions), so our description of folk religion refers generally to the traditional patterns which were prominent until the late nineteenth century.

Folk Religion in Family, Village, and Occupation

Just as there is no single religion called "Japanese religion," so is there no simple entity called "Japanese folk religion." Rather, folk religion exists implicitly within the informal settings such as family, village, and occupation. Each setting, in its own way, participates in the little tradition of Japanese religion and serves to transmit it to the next generation, both by word of mouth and by direct example.

The family itself is an important religious institution in Japan. Even in terms of organized religion, the traditional home is a center of Buddhist worship by virtue of the presence of the *butsudan* (Buddhist altar for the ancestors), and also a center of Shinto worship by virtue of the presence of the *kamidana* (god-shelf). But the family and home do not gain their religious character merely by borrowing from organized religion; rather they seem to have a religious character which precedes and stands apart from organized religion. As one scholar has put it, "certain types of psychological security found in a relationship to a personal God in the West are found only in relation to the actual family in Japan."[2] The traditional Japanese identified membership in the family with his sense of belonging in the world. The family as a religious institution has at least three levels: the ancestors, semidivine figures who are memorialized and grant blessings; the living, who perform the memorial rites and receive blessings; and the unborn, who eventually are the link between the ancestors and living, and the future. This important function of the family was never fully expressed by organized religion, but usually was maintained within the loose set of beliefs and customs known as folk religion.

The religious activities centering in the home had their own rhythmic unity. Traditionally most homes practiced memorial rites for the family dead, especially on the monthly and annual death anniversaries of the immediate family ancestors. Also, daily offerings, especially food from the family table, might be placed on the *kamidana*. In addition, there were important annual celebrations at the home, such as New Year's. Without any priestly help the family would consecrate the house for New Year's: Usually a pine branch was placed on the gate, or a pine tree was erected in the yard. In the entry way a special New Year's decoration of cooked rice was customary. In the countryside there were distinctive New Year's foods, such as the specially prepared New Year's soup, and the pounded glutinous rice. In olden times it was the custom to purify the house at the end of the year by a thorough cleaning, including the use of salt and sacred water; in many locales the hearth was extinguished and a new fire was obtained from a nearby temple or shrine. New Year's is only one example of the family's informal religious heritage.

The village is a larger setting in which folk religion is expressed and handed down. A village or sometimes a larger region shares a special myth or legend which is preserved in the memory of the people and is celebrated by one or more groups, often in connection with distinctive customs. An example of one legend and its observation may serve as an illustration of this kind of folk religion. In one locale of northern Japan there is a legend that in ancient times the people were bothered by a poisonous insect; eventually the insect was driven away by the performance of a ritual in which a mock insect made of straw was burned.

---

[2]George DeVos, quoted in David W. Plath, "Where the Family of God is the Family: The Role of the Dead in Japanese Households," p. 307. This article is abridged in H. Byron Earhart, *Religion in the Japanese Experience*, pp. 148–54.

According to one version it was an imperial prince who first began the ritual; in another version the ritual was revealed to the daughter of a Shinto priest. (In folk religion there is no one true version, as in a written scripture.) Every year the ritual is performed and before the mock insect is burned, sections of large straw rope around the mock insect are thrown among the youth of the village who try to grab one. The pieces of rope are said to represent the "bones" of the insect, and are taken home by the youths who hang them under the eaves of the house. Not only is the ritual said to drive away the insects, but the rope sections are believed to prevent fires in the homes where they are displayed.

This is but one example of many local beliefs and practices which continue in the lives of the people with very little help from organized religion. Almost every village in every district makes claim to some more or less distinctive legend and its celebration. The legend may connect a mythological figure to the locale and an annual festival, or it may have to do with the economic life of the region. Often special crafts and rather distinctive foods are involved in the celebration of such legends.

Folk beliefs and practices are also closely tied to occupations. Fishermen ③ with smaller wooden boats have special rites to drive out the spirit of the trees in a newly built boat, at the same time invoking a spirit of the sea. A small altar is often placed by the mast of the boat and offerings are made at the altar. This spirit helps protect against drowning and gives large catches, but it is offended by the presence of women and Buddhist priests, who usually are not allowed aboard these boats. Traditional lumbermen had their own rites for pacifying the spirit of a tree they cut down, and they observed various taboos within their mountain lodges. Certain words offended the tree spirits, and while in the mountains the lumbermen had to use a special "mountain language" when referring to the tabooed terms.

A widespread folk tradition among rice farmers was the notion that the *kami* of the rice field alternated with the *kami* of a nearby hill or mountain. Each spring the mountain *kami* descended the mountain and became the rice field *kami* for the duration of the growing season, and in the fall ascended in the smoke of the rice straw to become once more the mountain *kami*. A number of regions have special celebrations in spring and fall to mark the movement of the *kami*. Rice farmers in some other regions hold the belief that the rice field *kami* resides in the family home during the winter. Most of these folk beliefs related to occupations have been strongest in the older traditional forms of work, and have tended to die out as work has become organized on a more impersonal, mass basis, as in factories.

The Individual and Folk Religion

There was never any uniform organization of folk religion, so it is the nature of folk religion to include several variations of the same local legend, and to have a variety of beliefs and practices related to the rice field *kami*. The family, village, and occupations are three major contexts in which this little tradition is handed down. The individual might participate in folk religion within all three of these contexts, and yet there were still other ways in which folk religion spoke directly to him or her. One such illustration is the notion of *yakudoshi*, unlucky or dangerous years in the life of an individual. These years were ages twenty-five, forty-two, and sixty-one for men, and ages nineteen, thirty-three, and thirty-seven for women. One had to be very careful during these critical years, and it was a very bad omen if during one's unlucky year an acquaintance of the same age became sick or died. To offset the ominous character of the critical age, it was customary to hold special celebrations for the unlucky person, in the hopes of bringing him good luck.

Not only did folk religion supply beliefs and practices for the ordinary individual, but also it provided specialists who ministered to his religious needs. The most conspicuous of these religious specialists was the traditional shaman, usually a blind woman who had undergone extensive training with another shaman and thereby was able to go into a trance and speak with the dead. In some periods these shamans were brought under indirect control of organized religion, but most of the time the shamans lived in ordinary homes within villages, carrying out their role of medium upon the request of another individual. Such shamans or mediums are still found in Japan today. The person making the request may be concerned about the well-being of a deceased relative, so he visits the shaman with the customary payment for her to act as medium with the dead. The shaman makes an offering to her guardian spirit, recites the liturgy and formulas she learned in her training, and thereby enters into a trance, so that the voice of the dead can speak through her mouth. The conversation between the grieving person and his dead relative is rather formal—how the dead relative is faring in the other world, and what offerings might make him happy. Nevertheless, this religious service, performed outside organized religion, speaks directly to the relationship between the living and dead, one of the most important aspects in all of Japanese religion. The significance of folk religion is demonstrated by this ability to work within the everyday ordinary contexts of daily life and yet minister directly to the crucial religious needs of the people.

SELECTED READINGS

Bownas, Geoffrey. *Japanese Rainmaking and Other Folk Practices.* Popular descriptions of folk religion and customs.

Dorson, Richard M. *Folk Legends of Japan.* A topical collection, with brief introductions for each tale.

Earhart, H. Byron. "The Celebration of *Haru-yama* (Spring Mountain): An Example of Folk Religious Practices in Contemporary Japan." Description of a mountain pilgrimage celebrating the coming of spring.

——. *Religion in the Japanese Experience.* See Part Six for selected documents on folk religion, including excerpts from Dorson, Hori, and Oto.

Fairchild, William P. "Shamanism in Japan." Contains information on the history and careers of Japanese shamanesses.

Hori, Ichiro. *Folk Religion in Japan.* The best general work on aspects of folk religion; see pp. 181–251 for a good summary of the dynamics of shamanism in Japan.

Miyake, Hitoshi. "Folk Religion," in *Japanese Religion*, edited by Ichiro Hori, pp. 121–43. A concise analysis of folk religion, describing its annual festivals, rites of passage, and social organization.

Oto, Tokihiko. *Folklore in Japanese Life and Customs.* Profusely illustrated with excellent drawings and photographs.

Ouwehand, C. *Namazu-e and Their Themes. An Interpretative Approach to Some Aspects of Japanese Folk Religion.* The most thorough and systematic treatment of Japanese folk religion in English, important for its holistic interpretation.

8.

Interaction in the Formation of Japanese Religion

Five Formative Traditions Within Japanese Religious History

We have now surveyed the major formative elements of Japanese religious history in their initial appearance. In addition to folk religion, at least five formative elements can be recognized: the earliest tradition, Shinto, Buddhism, Confucianism, and religious Taoism. We have seen how all these religious traditions interacted to create a common religious milieu participated in and shared by the Japanese people. In other words, the five religious traditions may be seen as the main ingredients from which Japanese religion was formed. To a certain extent they maintained their individual identities, but for the most part they were interdependent in the forming of Japanese religion. They were not the total ingredients, because in later periods there appeared new currents of these same religious traditions. Especially the traditions of continental origin received new stimuli from successive importations. Buddhism experienced several waves of new influence. Religious Taoism was reimported to Japan in conjunction with the wave of esoteric Buddhism. Confucianism was strengthened by the later intrusions of Neo-Confucianism, which was intimately connected with the later waves of Zen Buddhism. Although the earliest (or indigenous) Japanese religious tradition and Shinto did not receive any new currents, they did undergo significant transformations.

However, the important thing to be noted is that we have now seen all the major traditions which contribute to Japanese religious history. After the Nara period new currents of the older traditions entered Japan, but (with the exception of Christianity) there were no new traditions. By this time all the major forces in the drama of Japanese religious history had made their first appearance, and the stage was set for the formation of a genuinely Japanese religion. Even at this early point in the historical drama we can see the future course of action. A general consideration of the five traditions will show their interaction and participation in a common religious milieu.

First we will observe the interaction of these five formative traditions. Anesaki used the statement attributed to Prince Shotoku to view the relationship of three of them:

> A saying ascribed to Prince Shotoku, the founder of Japanese civilization, compares the three religious and moral systems found in Japan to the root, the stem and branches, and the flowers and fruits of a tree. Shinto is the root embedded in the soil

of the people's character and national traditions; Confucianism is seen in the stem and branches of legal institutions, ethical codes, and educational systems; Buddhism made the flowers of religious sentiment bloom and gave the fruits of spiritual life. These three systems were moulded and combined by the circumstances of the times and by the genius of the people into a composite whole of the nation's spiritual and moral life.[1]

This traditional interpretation of Japanese religion may not have been made by Shotoku, but it is perceptive of the actual situation.[2] For historical accuracy we might add two other traditions to this threefold metaphor without radically changing it: the indigenous Japanese religious tradition, and religious Taoism. We might say that the earliest (or indigenous) tradition is the native soil in which the roots grow, supporting the tree. Similarly, we might say that religious Taoism is imperceptibly mixed in the sap of the tree, being absorbed into the three traditions of Buddhism, Confucianism, and Shinto, even seeping into the surrounding soil. Perhaps this metaphor, in its expanded version, gives a useful overall picture of what is meant in this book by the interrelatedness of Japanese religion. (Even folk religion and the New Religions, although not fully developed in this early period, fit well into the same metaphor. Folk religion may be seen as the "leafing out" of the tree into full foliage, while the New Religions can be viewed as the new sprouts which emerge after the tree has temporarily died back.)

Interaction in the Formation of Japanese Religion

Next we should point out some specific areas in which these various traditions mutually contributed to the formation of Japanese religion. One area is the so-called ancestor worship. Even in prehistoric times there was special veneration of the dead, possibly the dead of particular clans. Shinto was soon relieved of funeral rites by Buddhism, but even today several important Shinto shrines still venerate the spirits of national heroes. Buddhism greatly emphasized veneration for the dead by means of regular memorial rites, just as Confucianism provided the ethical rationale of filial piety. (Taoism seems to have played no important role in this area.) Therefore, whether we maintain the older term ancestor worship or adopt a new term such as veneration for the dead, this typical expression of Japanese religion must be seen as the total product of most of the formative traditions.

A second area, closely related to ancestor worship, is the religious continuity of the family, living and dead. Many important shrines and temples in early Japan

---

[1]Masaharu Anesaki, *History of Japanese Religion*, p. 8.

[2]See Ryusaku Tsunoda, *et al., Sources of Japanese Tradition*, Chapter 13, where this passage is traced to the writings of Yoshida Kanetomo (1435–1511), and a different interpretation is given; Yoshida's purpose for writing it is to demonstrate the primacy of Shinto over Buddhism and Confucianism: "Thus all foreign doctrines are offshoots of Shinto."

were the private sanctuaries of separate clans. Affiliation with Shinto shrines was usually determined either by blood relationship or geographical boundaries. Families became linked to a specific Buddhist temple through the regular memorials to family ancestors. Confucianism generally stressed social harmony and lines of obedience in the family and country at large. Thus, although there was no one social body, all the formative traditions stressed social solidarity of the Japanese people.

A third area in which these traditions shared was the close tie between nation and religion which has characterized most of Japanese history. In this sense all social groups were united in the nation, with religious stimulus from all the formative traditions. The earliest religious tradition was only weakly in favor of a centrally unified religion and state—partly because the clans combined a political and religious leader in their own clan chiefs. Shinto attempted to raise the status of the emperor by the mythological account of his divine descent from the Sun Goddess, and was supported by both Buddhism and Confucianism. Buddhism practically became a state religion which protected the ruler and his realm, while Confucianism provided the notion of a Son of Heaven with a divine mandate. Religious Taoism, represented by the divination bureau, promised the proper foundation of nation and society on the basis of cosmic harmony.

Several other areas of Japanese religion which demonstrate manifold influence from the five traditions can be summed up more briefly. These areas are: pluralism of religions and religious beliefs, emphasis on magical procedures, and religious sentiment in a love of nature. Pluralism has always been a conspicuous feature of Japanese religion. There have been incidents of antagonism between the religious traditions, but they are the exception rather than the rule. Usually it has not been the case that any one religious tradition thought of itself as the true religion to the exclusion of other (false) religions. (Later we will see that the Nichiren sect of Buddhism is an important exception to this general rule.) One tradition presupposed the existence of the other traditions, and either consciously or unconsciously borrowed from the other traditions. Only in this kind of atmosphere could they contribute commonly to ancestor worship and the religious support of the state. And only in this atmosphere could the people participate simultaneously in all the traditions. It is true that the common people might not be self-conscious of an indigenous tradition nor of religious Taoism, and might not give second thought to Confucianism. But even when they could see some superficial differences between Buddhism and Shinto, they accepted the two traditions as similar or complementary. It was only natural that the Buddha was first seen by the Japanese people as a foreign *kami*. Later, as Buddhism became more Japanized, Buddhist divinities were worshiped by all with the same fervor that was directed towards the native kami.

Magical formulas and charms have been characteristic of Japanese religion, as supported by all the traditions. For example, Taoistic charms have been adopted by both Shinto and Buddhism. In fact, Buddhism was accepted in Japan because its magical efficacy was believed to surpass that of Shinto. Similarly, shamanistic possession or trance has been recorded in the indigenous tradition, Shinto, and Buddhism.

Love of nature is a distinctive feature of the Japanese spirit, and can be seen (6) in most artistic and religious expressions, although it is difficult to define. The earliest picture of Japan in the poetry anthology *Manyoshu*, and also in the early Shinto rituals, shows a refined appreciation of the religious and creative resources in the natural world. For the sake of contrast we might say that in the Western tradition the tendency has been to define both God and man apart from nature; in Japan both *kami* and man are defined in relation to nature or as a part of nature. The Japanese appreciation of nature is found not only within the earliest religious tradition in Japan and Shinto, but is reinforced by the other traditions. The whole aim of religious Taoism's many practices was to be in harmony with nature, and Confucianism drew on this natural harmony for its insistence on social harmony. Buddhism's openness to the natural world later was developed into a return to nature by the Zen sect, which already had received Taoist influence in China.

This brief survey of the cooperation among the five formative traditions is not an exhaustive analysis of Japanese religion, but does provide a basis for understanding its nature and development in the subsequent centuries. These basic elements continued to interact with each other while developing specific religious organizations and while contributing to the wider religious situation. The appearance of new religious currents, particularly Buddhist importation, was of great importance in determining the way in which these elements interacted.

(By the end of the eighth century CE)

SELECTED READINGS

Earhart, H. Byron. *Religion in the Japanese Experience.* See Part Eight for selected documents on syncretism in Japan; see pp. 39–44 for excerpts from Matsunaga.

Kamstra, J. H. *Encounter or Syncretism. The Initial Growth of Japanese Buddhism.* A technical and detailed study of syncretism, analyzing the early career of Buddhism in Japan.

Matsunaga, Alicia. *The Buddhist Philosophy of Assimilation.* Treats the interaction between aspects of Buddhism and aspects of Japanese culture.

Nakamura, Hajime. *Ways of Thinking of Eastern Peoples.* The section on Japan, pp. 345–587, deals with the common thought and belief patterns which form the basis for interaction among the several religious traditions.

Part II

THE DEVELOPMENT
AND ELABORATION
OF JAPANESE
RELIGION

9.

The Founding of a Japanese Buddhism: The Tendai and Shingon Sects

The New Buddhism of the Heian Period

By the end of the eighth century, the major outlines of Japanese religion were taking shape. We saw in Part I that the major formative elements had appeared and begun their characteristic cooperation toward creating a common religious atmosphere. From this point on, there occurred a development and elaboration of these earlier elements. The direction which this development and elaboration took was determined mainly by two factors: first, the general patterns which took shape in the formative period and which were continued in this second period; second, the waves of new influence on the basic traditions discussed in Part I.

In general, the major innovation of the second period, covering the ninth through the sixteenth centuries, was the reimportation of Buddhism from China and the repercussions therefrom. Most of the religious developments during this time depended on, or were directly connected with, the new Buddhist currents. For example, both religious Taoism and (later) Neo-Confucianism were reintroduced to Japan through the channel of Buddhism. In addition, even the transformation of Shinto into specific schools depended on new Buddhist (and Taoistic) theories. In Part II we will see how Buddhism received several new continental influences and elaborated older themes into larger proportions. Shinto continued to maintain its older heritage, while becoming increasingly organized along Buddhist and Taoistic lines. For the most part religious Taoism and Confucianism persevered as implicit influences rather than as distinct traditions. Christianity was the only new tradition to appear within this period.

The first major factor to be considered is the new Buddhism which dominated the Heian period (794–1185). Older Buddhism, meaning the six philosophical schools of the Nara period (710–784), was mainly the religion of the nobility and the monks, and had become more and more corrupt with its increasing wealth and power. Therefore, it is only natural to expect that a reform movement would take place. It is important to understand how the reform of Buddhism occurred, because it colored the whole Heian period and influenced much of later Japanese religious history.

Politically, the Heian period was ushered in by the shift of the capital from Nara to Kyoto, which remained the imperial capital until 1868. It is thought that one reason for moving the capital from Nara was the intolerable corruption and the political interference of the older six schools of Nara Buddhism. This move freed the capital from the grip of Nara Buddhism and set up the possibility for a reform of Buddhism. Religiously, the Heian period is distinguished by two new Buddhist sects, each of which was founded by an outstanding religious leader. The Shingon sect was founded by Kukai (774–835), known posthumously as Kobo Daishi. The Tendai sect was founded by Saicho (762–822), honored posthumously as Dengyo Daishi. (*Daishi* is an honorary term meaning "great teacher.")

The two sects and their founders share many features in common. Not only were the founders contemporaries, but they went to China by imperial sanction at the same time in their quest of an authoritative Buddhism. Both were Buddhist priests who, dissatisfied with Nara Buddhism, traveled to China in search of the true Buddhism. Even more important, both seem to have been committed to the ideal of establishing a genuinely *Japanese* Buddhism. That is, they wanted actively to propagate a kind of Buddhism which would provide all the Japanese people with the teachings of Buddhism. We will also see some important differences between the two movements. For example, the two founders differed in their choice of sects of Buddhism in China, and in their organization of the sects upon their return to Japan.

Shingon: Esoteric Buddhism in Japan

Kobo Daishi, the founder of Shingon, is one of the most illustrious figures in Japanese history. Although highly revered for founding the Shingon sect, he was popularly honored as the creator of the Japanese phonetic system of writing, and still is venerated in many places he is supposed to have visited. However, his historical significance is best seen in his transmission of esoteric Buddhism from China to Japan. During Kobo Daishi's stay in China (804–806), he learned all there was to know of esoteric Buddhism, obtaining the crucial Buddhist scriptures (in Chinese translation) and ritual paraphernalia.

It is well to remember that esoteric Buddhism had its origin in the Tantric tradition of India which came to fruition about the third to seventh centuries A.D. Both Hinduism and Buddhism received Tantric influence, which emphasized highly symbolic and often secret formulas, rituals, and gestures. Tantric scriptures and practices usually aimed at orienting a person within the cosmos or identifying him with a divinity.[1] Tantric Buddhism came directly from India to China where it was quickly translated, but there was too little time for a thorough Chinese transformation of esoteric Buddhism. This highly ritualistic aspect of Buddhism became the vogue in China about the eighth century, and was known by the sect name of Chen-yen in Chinese (meaning "true word," or Shingon in Japanese pronunciation). Nevertheless, the formal tradition of esoteric Buddhism in China (the Chen-yen sect) did not survive a severe persecution in the year 845 A.D.

Kobo Daishi's transplantation of the esoteric Buddhist tradition was a radically new contribution of Buddhism to Japan, one which was more strongly Indian than Chinese. If Kobo Daishi brought a new Buddhism to Japan, equally important is what he did with it on Japanese soil. He dissociated himself both from the old Buddhism of Nara and from the new capital, to establish a monastery on the secluded mountain called Koyasan. In part, Kobo Daishi imitated the mountain monasteries of China, but also he emphasized the need to make Buddhism native to Japan. Even though he established his esoteric tradition far from the capital, the esoteric doctrines—and especially the rites—soon were sought after by both laity and priests.

Shingon teaching divides Buddhism into the exoteric or public, and the esoteric or secret. Exoteric or public teachings are not wrong, but limited to inferior knowledge; by contrast, the esoteric or secret teaching reveals the heart of the cosmos and enables one to draw upon this higher power. The key to the esoteric knowledge is the *Great Sun Sutra* (*Mahavairocana Sutra* in Sanskrit, *Dainichi-kyo* in Japanese), which constitutes a basic scripture for Shingon. In this scripture is the description of the cosmos as an emanation from the Sun Buddha (Vairocana, or Dainichi in Japanese). The esoteric knowledge of Shingon reveals the higher unity in the Sun Buddha which transcends the apparent dualities in the world. Ordinarily we experience this life in terms of dualities such as male and female, dynamic and static; Shingon speaks of this duality as the diamond and womb aspects of the world. In the ordinary view of the world it appears hopelessly split, but the "esoteric" knowledge of Shingon reveals that there is a higher unity of all things within their original source in the Sun Buddha. All the doctrine, art, and ritual of Shingon is based on this crucial premise of the Sun Buddha as the original source of the cosmos.

Shingon doctrine, because of its highly symbolic and esoteric character, is one of the most complex in all of Japanese Buddhism. It is easier for the average

---

[1]For a brief treatment of Tantric Buddhism, see Edward Conze, *Buddhism: Its Essence and Development* (New York: Harper & Brothers, 1959), pp. 174–99.

layman and Westerner to grasp the artistic expressions of Shingon. The two aspects of the world are often expressed in two contrasting world pictures of *mandala* (in Sanskrit), symbolic representations of the cosmos. With the popularization of Buddhist art these *mandala* are often seen in the West: Usually they feature a square border enclosing symmetrical patterns of squares within circles and circles within squares. Literally hundreds of Buddhist divinities are found within these smaller circles and squares, each identified by its particular iconographic attributes and mystic gestures. (Sometimes the divinities are represented, instead, by the mystic letters associated with them.) Such a *mandala* presents an impressive, overwhelming panorama of the Buddhist cosmos. The *mandala* were sometimes used in Shingon ordination rites: The blindfolded priest threw a flower on the *mandala*, and thereby became directly linked with the particular Buddhist divinity on which the flower fell. There was also the practice of meditating upon the *mandala*, and thereby uniting one's own life with the higher cosmic truth.

Even for the average person who did not perform these more difficult practices, merely to behold the splendor of the *mandala* was to be given a glimpse of the cosmic vision to which Shingon held the key. The same can be said of the fearful statues of Shingon, which to Western eyes appear grotesque. These statues feature menacing countenance, glaring eyes, sharp teeth, and brandished weapon. But they are simply the malevolent side of various deities, the counterpart of the benevolent side. Shingon in its quest for total cosmic vision does not attempt to deny the evil and violence in the world, but seeks first to comprehend the actual duality within the world and then to affirm the higher unity that transcends worldly duality. Although the people would not necessarily comprehend the full plan of the cosmic vision, they readily brought devotion and offerings to these awesome statues.

The dynamics of Shingon are found within her great ritual treasures. Kobo Daishi brought back from China both ritual paraphernalia and the actual liturgies for performing the rituals. Immediately Kobo Daishi and his followers were in demand for performing rites at the court. Especially popular with the court were rites for healing and for such occasions as childbirth. Rather quickly such rites came to be practiced by all Buddhist priests as requests came from the court and nobility, and eventually from the people. Perhaps the most fascinating of all Shingon rituals is its fire rite called *goma*, which is thought to be related to the Indian *soma* sacrifice. In the *goma* rite the priest builds up layers of wood and ignites it, pouring on it various substances such as sesame oil. (In Japanese sesame is *goma*.) The symbolism of the rite includes the basic elements of the universe, burning defilements and purifying the self, and becoming transported by the wisdom of fire to the higher truth of Shingon. To sit in a dark temple, listening to the chanting of the priest, and watching the flames leap up, illuminating the gilded statues, is indeed an experience which elevates the viewer to another world.

This quest for cosmic power in Shingon may appear foreign to early Buddhism, but it was totally consistent with Tantric Buddhism. The Indian bent for elaborate iconography and complex symbolism in doctrine and ritual is reflected more within Shingon Buddhism than in any other form of Japanese Buddhism. In fact, Shingon is much closer to the esoteric Buddhism of Tibet, with which it shares the common historical foundation of Tantric Buddhism, than to other sects of Japanese Buddhism. However, the principle that Buddhism provides power for solving immediate problems was accepted as soon as Buddhism reached Japanese shores: The first arguments for and against Buddhism were framed in terms of whether Buddhism held such power. But in the Nara period Buddhism consisted mainly of philosophical schools, and possessed only fragments of the esoteric tradition. The major contribution of Kobo Daishi was to bring to Japan the whole range of the esoteric art, doctrine, and ritual in a systematic form. He even developed an all-embracing philosophy of religion which established a critique of all the then known religions on a hierarchical scale of ten levels, with esoteric Buddhism occupying the highest level.

This overview of Shingon helps us understand the tremendous contribution of Shingon to Japanese Buddhism. For the aesthetically inclined, the artistic expressions and elaborate rituals were overwhelming. For the intellectual there was a comprehensive system explaining the nature of the world and criticizing all other known philosophical systems. The devotionally minded could utilize the meditation, divinities, and ritual as acts of personal fulfillment to experience the unity of this cosmic vision in his own life. For magical purposes the many magical formulas of Shingon provided easy access to cosmic power. So attractive were these dramatic aspects of Shingon that they were quickly borrowed and used by the other Buddhist sects, and gradually filtered down to the people. However, Shingon did not generate new Buddhist sects in the fashion of Tendai, the other major Buddhist sect in the Heian period.

Tendai: Faith in the Lotus Sutra and Amida as the Watershed of Japanese Buddhist Sects

The Tendai sect founded by Dengyo Daishi became increasingly more important than the Shingon sect after the Heian period. Historically, Tendai can be considered the more important of the two sects, since Dengyo Daishi's sect spawned most of the later Buddhist developments within Japanese history. Although Dengyo Daishi went to China at the same time as Kobo Daishi, his experience there was quite different. Dengyo Daishi viewed the Chinese form of esoteric Buddhism merely as one important Buddhist tradition along with Ch'an (the Chinese term for the Zen sect). For Dengyo Daishi the T'ien-t'ai sect was superior to the other Buddhist traditions. Dengyo Daishi spent most of his time in China at the headquarters of the T'ien-t'ai sect, on a mountain called by the same name of T'ien-t'ai. (Tendai is the Japanese pronunciation of T'ien-t'ai.) One of Dengyo Daishi's cherished projects was to establish an official ordination altar in Japan modeled after a Chinese Buddhist altar, but due to the objections of other Buddhist sects, the state did not grant permission for erection of such an altar until several years after his death.

The central scripture of Tendai is the Lotus Sutra, which is considered as the culmination of the Buddha's teaching. Originally the Chinese monk Chih-i (538-597) established the T'ien-t'ai sect around the doctrine of the Lotus Sutra. Theoretically all doctrines flow from the Lotus Sutra, but in actuality the founder Chih-i borrowed the teachings of the great Buddhist scholar Nagarjuna to found his doctrine. This doctrine is a complicated threefold analysis of existence whose significance is a radical denial of phenomenal existence and at the same time a radical acceptance of phenomenal existence.[2] For the layman this means that even his daily life, if properly perceived and meditated on, can be the road to Buddhahood (becoming Buddha or attaining the level of a Buddha). In both China and Japan the Tendai sect emphasized that no Buddhist practice is valid without the proper meditation.

When Dengyo Daishi returned to Japan he went back to the mountain called Hieizan, overlooking the new capital of Kyoto. There he established the Tendai sect, emphasizing the Lotus Sutra and retreat for proper meditation. Of course, the Lotus Sutra already had a considerable history in Japan, since even Prince Shotoku is supposed to have written a commentary on it, and the older Buddhist schools of Nara recognized its profundity. Dengyo Daishi's contribution, however, was to teach the primary importance of the Lotus Sutra. He criticized earlier interpretations of the Lotus Sutra as false, and proposed as the true interpretation that "all forms of life stand on an equal basis in attaining Buddhahood."[3] Dengyo Daishi was uncompromising, not only on doctrinal matters, but also in matters of training and ordination. His criticism of corrupt Nara Buddhism and his concern for proper meditation led him to prescribe a twelve-year period of training for monks on Hieizan, during which time they were not allowed to leave the mountain. His insistence on establishing the proper rite of ordination (which he already had received in China and now wanted to install in Japan) involved him in a lifelong struggle. Under his guidance Hieizan became the center of Buddhist studies in Japan.

The mountain headquarters of Hieizan symbolizes Dengyo Daishi's great plans for Japanese Buddhism. He was concerned that Buddhism in Japan be orthodox in ordination rites, scriptures, doctrine, and devotion. Having received proper ordination himself (in China), he felt qualified to lead orthodox Buddhism in Japan. Convinced that the Lotus Sutra was the essential teaching of Buddhism, he upheld it as the foremost scripture. For doctrine he transmitted the T'ien-t'ai teachings based on the Lotus Sutra, that every phenomenal aspect of the world is filled with Buddha nature. Determined that his monks be properly devout and disciplined, he required long periods of meditation. History rewarded Dengyo Daishi's efforts, for Hieizan became the monastic and scholastic headquarters of all Japanese Buddhism, regardless of sect affiliation. In spite of the ravages of time

---

[2]For a brief interpretation of this Tendai doctrine, see Ryusaku Tsunoda, et al., *Sources of Japanese Tradition*, Chapter 6.

[3]Shinsho Hanayama, "Buddhism in Japan," p. 325.

II. DEVELOPMENT AND ELABORATION

and warfare, much of the glory of this monastic headquarters survives today, and is a popular tourist attraction just outside Kyoto. One of the peculiar architectural structures at Hieizan is the chapel with an image of Amida in the center of an empty room, so that priests could circumambulate Amida while in devotional meditation.

The impact of Tendai on popular life is not so clear as that of Shingon. One of Tendai's greatest contributions is the placing of the Lotus Sutra in the center of attention, for this is probably the single most influential Buddhist scripture for China and Japan. In the Lotus Sutra we find the most direct and dramatic expression of the gist of Mahayana Buddhism: All beings may easily attain enlightenment through simple acts of devotion. In the words of the Lotus Sutra, whoever memorizes or recites but a single stanza of this scripture "and who honours that book with flowers, incense, perfumed garlands, ointment, powder, clothes, umbrellas, flags, banners, music, joined hands, reverential bows and salutations . . . must be held to be accomplished in supreme and perfect enlightenment."[4] This compassionate rendering of Buddhism summed up the meaning of the tradition to the majority of the Japanese people. Tendai teaching so emphasized the penetration of Buddha-nature within the phenomenal world that in medieval times it preached the inherent Buddha nature of the natural world. "Not only the grass and trees but also rivers, mountains, and the earth are themselves Buddhahood already possessed intact."[5] Here we see how the Japanese concern for the natural world became part of Tendai teaching.

The founders of the Shingon and Tendai sects were contemporaries, but they led different careers and made contrasting contributions to Japanese Buddhism. Some scholars feel that Dengyo Daishi would have been more successful if he had been more compromising, like Kobo Daishi. Both men founded headquarters of mountain Buddhism in Japan, and yet their fortunes were quite different. Kobo Daishi's fame was immediate and lasting, while his sect was of only relative importance for religious history, as a covert influence. On the other hand, Dengyo Daishi has enjoyed less personal fame, but his sect is of the utmost importance for subsequent religious history as the source of all later Buddhist sects. Two elements which Dengyo Daishi brought to Japan along with Tendai were faith in the *bodhisattva* named Amida, and Zen practices. For a while these two elements enjoyed only a minor role within Tendai, especially because Tendai itself became heavily laden with Shingon ritualistic influence. Gradually Tendai developed its own esoteric (Mikkyo) tradition. However, with the passing of Shingon's golden age, these two dormant elements woke to new life. They became so active that they burst the bonds of Tendai and formed new sects. Before going on to

---

[4] *Saddharma-Pundarika or The Lotus of the True Law*, translated by H. Kern (The Sacred Books of the East, Vol. XX; Reprinted, New York: Dover Publications, 1963). See p. 215. An excerpt from this scripture is in H. Byron Earhart, *Religion in the Japanese Experience*, pp. 44–47.

[5] Hajime Nakamura, *Ways of Thinking of Eastern Peoples*, p. 360.

9. The Founding of a Japanese Buddhism   *55*

discuss these new Buddhist sects, it is well to note some general characteristics of the Heian period.

The Development of Japanese Buddhism and Japanese Religion

The Heian period was a strong affirmation of the Japanese creative ability to mold to its own taste the innumerable continental borrowings. Nara Buddhism had remained in essence a foreign religion. Kobo Daishi and Dengyo Daishi were agreed at least on the reason for searching out the authoritative Buddhism in China: to mold it into a truly Japanese Buddhism. The same might be said about the arts. Most of the earlier art either had been brought from the continent or directly copied from continental examples. However, from about the ninth to twelfth centuries intercourse with China was broken off, partly due to political turmoil in China. Another explanation for this cessation of missions to China was a reaction against Chinese influence. As a result, Japanese culture in general—including religion and art—was allowed to develop in its own manner. It was a glorious time for the arts, and we can see that Shingon managed to thrive both as a sect and as an underground influence, whereas its Chinese counterpart Chen-yen soon faded out of the picture. We might say that Japanese culture had come of age.

For Japanese Buddhism this meant that Buddhism, too, took on a decidedly Japanese character. At the outset of this chapter we indicated that the period of development and elaboration was characterized by two trends: the continuation of general patterns that took shape in the formative period, and the appearance of new waves of influence such as the new Buddhism. Thus far we have surveyed only the new waves of influence. But even the new character of Tendai and Shingon did not mean a discontinuity with the general patterns of Japanese religion that emerged in the formative period. On the contrary, it should be pointed out that Tendai and Shingon reinforced those earlier religious patterns. Both Shingon and Tendai deliberately emphasized the Japanese character of Buddhism. Both the Shingon and Tendai headquarters were founded with full cooperation of the *kami* who were considered the patron deities of these two mountains. Thus, the rapport between the Buddhas and *kami* became even more intimate. The Tendai and Shingon sects also tended to spread Buddhist teachings and build temples in areas distant from the capital.

In addition, although these two new sects had reacted to the state Buddhism of Nara, eventually both the ritualism of Shingon and the ecclesiastical authority of Tendai were used to protect and bless the state. The artistic and magical heritage of esoteric Buddhism and the Tendai emphasis on the Lotus Sutra gradually blended with the characteristically Japanese emphasis on purification and ritualism. Many Buddhist divinities (*bodhisattvas*), such as Kannon, Amida, and Jizo, became increasingly important as objects of popular piety. These magical charms and Buddhist divinities were not confined to organized Buddhism—

temples and priests—but became the living faith of the people. "All through the Nara and Heian periods, almost all the sects of Buddhism aimed at tangible rewards in this world and they mainly depended upon incantation and magic."[6] All in all, the Heian period saw Buddhism take on a decidedly Japanese character as it increasingly penetrated the life of the people.

Meanwhile, the earlier religious elements described in Part I actually coexisted alongside the new sects. In fact, the beliefs of religious Taoism were more active in the Heian than any other period. Medieval novels such as the famous *Tale of Genji* show how the movements of the people were determined by the "unlucky directions" learned from religious Taoism. The age was pervaded by all the implications of the *yin-yang* cosmology. The charms and incantations of earlier Buddhism, reinforced by both Shingon and its Taoistic coloring, penetrated all classes of society. The seventh-century precedent of having Buddhist priests perform burial services had become widespread. The Buddhist festival of *bon* for honoring the return of souls of the dead, probably with the help of ancient Japanese practices, became a popular festival throughout the country. Various religious practitioners—diviners, exorcists, ascetics—drew on all the previous traditions to serve the religious needs of the people. Shinto became more fully organized, as was evidenced by the compilation of the *Engishiki* of 927, but tended to lean on the prestige of Buddhism. The many *kami* of Shinto became even more closely identified with the Buddhas and *bodhisattvas*, and we will see that Shinto became organized around the complex philosophies of religious Taoism, Shingon, and Tendai. Folk religion showed its vitality, too. All of these elements became related to each other.

An example of the uniquely Japanese interrelationship of all these elements is the movement called Shugendo, a religious movement little known in the West. Shugendo became highly organized during and after the Heian period. Building on the ancient theme of sacred mountains and festivals performed on mountains, Shugendo developed a "mountain religion" which emphasized pilgrimage to the mountains and ascetic retreats within the mountains. It combined the Shinto notion of local *kami* dwelling on mountains with the Buddhist notion of local incarnations of Buddhas or *bodhisattvas*. In addition, it borrowed the theories and charms of religious Taoism. The legendary founder of Shugendo gained religious power by combining the aspects of several traditions: He practiced Buddhist asceticism on a Japanese sacred mountain while taking over features of the Chinese mountain wizard (*hsien* in Chinese, *sennin* in Japanese). Many of the previously mentioned popular religious practitioners gained their religious powers by training in the mountains, before descending to minister to the people. In later periods, while Shingon languished as a separate sect, Shugendo practitioners (called *yamabushi*) were instrumental in spreading the charms and incantations of esoteric Buddhism (mixed with Taoistic charms and Shinto elements)

---

[6]Hajime Nakamura, *Ways of Thinking of Eastern Peoples*, p. 363.

9. The Founding of a Japanese Buddhism   *57*

to the people. The *yamabushi* were important in spreading Buddhism to the people of northern Japan. This is but one illustration of the complex religious interrelationships within this period and later periods.

SELECTED READINGS

Earhart, H. Byron. *A Religious Study of the Mount Haguro Sect of Shugendo.* A detailed study of one Shugendo sect, treating the relationship of esoteric Buddhism to folk practices.

Hakeda, Yoshito S., trans. *Kukai: Major Works.* A scholarly introduction to the life and thought of the founder of Shingon Buddhism, with translations of his works.

Hori, Ichiro. "On the Concept of *Hijiri* (Holy-man)." Relates the *hijiri* to esoteric Buddhism and religious Taoism.

Hurvitz, Leon Nahum. *Chih-i (538–97); An Introduction to the Life and Ideas of a Chinese Buddhist Monk.* A detailed account of the founder of T'ien-t'ai (Tendai) Buddhism.

Kitagawa, Joseph M. "Master and Saviour." A valuable biography of Kobo Daishi, emphasizing his significance for popular religion.

Petzold, Bruno. "The Chinese Tendai Teaching." An analysis of Tendai philosophy in China and Japan.

Sansom, Sir George. *A History of Japan*, Vol. I, pp. 129–38. Provides a good description of the artistic and religious glory of Heian times.

Saunders, E. Dale. *Mudra. A Study of Symbolic Gestures in Japanese Buddhist Sculpture.* A detailed study of the artistic expression of esoteric Buddhism (and Buddhist sculpture in general), with profuse illustrations.

Tsunoda, Ryusaku, *et al. Sources of Japanese Tradition.* See Chapter 6 for translated documents concerning Tendai, and Chapter 7 for translated documents concerning Shingon.

Ui, Hakuju. "A Study of Japanese Tendai Buddhism." A detailed analysis of Tendai doctrine, comparing its Chinese origins with its Japanese developments.

10.
Elaboration Within Japanese Buddhism: The Pure Land, Nichiren, and Zen Sects

From Heian Buddhism to Kamakura Buddhism

It is ironic, but perhaps inevitable, that the Tendai and Shingon sects degenerated into the same kind of wealthy decadence against which they had revolted. The Shingon and Tendai sects arose out of a critique against the six schools of Nara —against their opulence, scholasticism, corruption, and spiritual ineffectiveness. Both Kobo Daishi and Dengyo Daishi founded their temple headquarters far enough from Nara so that they could withdraw from the contemporary corruption. Both founders proposed the ideal of a moral corrective on Buddhism by establishing rather secluded centers of devotion: the ritual of Shingon and the meditation of Tendai.

Nevertheless, to the degree that they were successful, these founders and the sects which outlived them inherited most of the faults of Nara Buddhism. The growing religious prestige of Tendai and Shingon earned them money from the nobility and power from the court. Kobo Daishi and his rituals were in great demand in all the temples of Heian times. Dengyo Daishi's personality brought him into conflict with many Buddhist leaders, but the wealth of his Tendai tradition and his advantageous location overlooking the new capital eventually made his sect the guardian of the state. The altar of ordination which he proposed became very important for later Buddhism, and he was the first Buddhist priest in Japan to receive the posthumous title of Daishi.

To sum up, these two sects paid for their success by becoming attached to their newly won wealth and power. Shingon rapidly became an elaborate ritualism for the sake of the wealthy. Tendai alternated between mountain meditation at Hieizan and political interference in the capital of Kyoto at the foot of Hieizan. Both sects split into smaller competing branches. It is no wonder that a critique should be raised against Shingon and Tendai, just as these sects had originally raised a critique against Nara Buddhism. Although the critique was made against both sects, it drew its strength mainly from the latent religious forces within Tendai.

In leaving the Heian period of relative peace we enter the troubled times of the Kamakura period (1185–1333). There was a main shift in political power from the court at Kyoto to ruling feudal powers headed by a generalissimo *(shogun)*.

*much
further
North*

The period draws its name from the site of Kamakura where this feudal government was first established. Actually, the struggles between rising feudal powers went back into the Heian period, but in the Kamakura period they dominated the whole scene. The large Buddhist temples also figured as major economic and military forces, contributing to the general unrest of the times.

The shift from the Heian period to the Kamakura period had two immediate consequences for Japanese Buddhism. First, the decline of the court and nobility tended to withdraw the patronage and financial support of Shingon and Tendai. Second, the uncertainty of life in these trying times called for a more immediate resolution of religious problems and man's salvation.

One of the Buddhist theories which resounded through this whole period was the theory of the "decline of the law." Here "law" (*dharma* in Sanskrit) has the meaning of Buddhism. This theory presupposed three major Buddhist ages of increasing degeneration: first, the ideal age when people followed the teaching of the Buddha and could attain enlightenment; second, a more degenerate age when people practiced the teaching of Buddha even though they knew enlightenment was impossible; and third, a completely degenerate age when no one even bothered to practice the Buddha's teachings. Japanese Buddhists, following the Chinese interpretation of this theory, understood that the first two ages were already past and they were living in the third and final age. The people who lived through the all too frequent warfare and bloodshed of the Kamakura period saw a parallel in this "final age" of Buddhist theory, and feared an imminent end of the world in the form of a great catastrophe. Moreover, they realized that in this age of the decline of the law, organized Buddhism itself was of little help to the layman in attaining immediate salvation.

This crisis within Buddhism, however, did not mean its extinction. On the contrary, even the philosophical schools of Nara and the Heian sects of Shingon and Tendai managed to survive. Furthermore, this new situation in Kamakura stimulated latent features within Japanese Buddhism. Buddhism flourished as never before. If the Heian period's contribution was an authentic *Japanese* Buddhism, then the Kamakura period's contribution was Buddhism for the Japanese *people.* The Kamakura developments of Buddhism marked the first time in Japanese history when Buddhism captured the attention of vast numbers of the common people, and it is these same movements that today claim the majority of Buddhist temples and Buddhist adherents. In Kamakura times Buddhism emphasized not so much the formal notion of enlightenment or salvation *(nirvana)* as the simpler religious goals such as rebirth into Amida's pure land.

Although neither Shingon nor Tendai could fully meet these new religious needs, it was Tendai that contained the germs for the three major Buddhist developments within Kamakura times. These three developments are the Pure Land sects, the Nichiren sect, and the Zen sects—three new kinds of sects which had not been represented at Nara. Each group of sects deserves separate treatment.

II. DEVELOPMENT AND ELABORATION

The Pure Land Sects: Faith in Amida and the Recitation of the *Nembutsu*

The term Pure Land (or Pure Realm) is a translation of the Japanese term Jodo. It can refer to one particular Buddhist sect, the Pure Land sect, but in a broader sense it refers to the Pure Land of Amida in the Buddhist pantheon. Amida (Amitabha or Amitayus in Sanskrit) was an important Buddha even in Indian Buddhism, becoming one of the most important objects of Buddhist devotion in China. Amida is depicted as having compassion on and wanting to save all human beings. To rescue them Amida brings humans to the heavenly paradise, otherwise called the Pure Land. All people can avail themselves of Amida's saving grace simply by invoking or chanting the name of Amida. In Japan this practice is known as *nembutsu:* the actual phrase is pronounced "namu Amida," or "namu Amida Butsu." This phrase means: "I put my faith in Amida Buddha." Originally the *nembutsu* meant meditation on Amida, but the element of meditation was soon replaced by fervent devotion and endless repetition. The rise of the Pure Land sects indicated this religious shift from meditation to faith. In China and then in Japan the cult of Amida became closely associated with memorials for the dead.

The simplicity of faith in Amida helped spread this cult throughout the land. While all the people yearned for their own salvation and the repose of their ancestors, only the few could spend the time and money for Shingon rituals and Tendai meditation. Furthermore, no comprehension of subtle doctrines was required in Pure Land Buddhism. Although the leading monks in the Pure Land sects were thoroughly trained in the monasteries of Hieizan and elsewhere, they emphasized the availability of salvation for even the illiterate peasant. Amida Buddhism did not win the day by an intellectual choice of Pure Land doctrine over Tendai and Shingon doctrine. It was not a matter of choosing one intellectual system over another intellectual system, but of choosing popular devotion to Amida over the former Buddhist systems. Faith in Amida became more important for the people than all the earlier Buddhist movements combined: the philosophical systems of Nara Buddhism, the rituals of Shingon, and the meditation of Tendai.

There were a number of Buddhist priests within the Tendai sect who stimulated belief in Amida, but the one who is most remembered as the founder of Pure Land as a separate sect is Honen (1133–1212). Most of the earlier priests who preached faith in Amida did so within the context of Tendai, without establishing a separate sect. The career of Honen is a good example of the changing religious atmosphere. Honen studied Buddhism at Hieizan during these tumultuous times and gained fame as a scholar. Nevertheless, even though he devoted his life to studying the many systems of Buddhist thought, he did not see how these complex doctrines could help a Japanese of the thirteenth century attain religious peace.

At the age of 42 he became convinced of the truth of the Pure Land teachings. In this he followed the Chinese masters of Pure Land teachings and his

Japanese forerunners. This new awareness of the truth of Pure Land teachings enabled Honen to make a clear distinction between the earlier Buddhist teachings in Japan and the newer teaching of faith in Amida. Here Honen followed the precedent of an earlier Japanese Amidist in calling the previous Buddhist teachings of right conduct and religious exercises the "holy path." The holy path he considered appropriate for the first two of the three stages of Buddhist history. However, for Honen who lived within the third and final stage, it was too much to expect that men could achieve salvation through their own efforts. The only hope for man in such evil times was the possibility of being reborn in Amida's Pure Land. Honen followed his Amidist forerunner in distinguishing sharply the overly "difficult" holy path of earlier sects and the need for an "easy" means of salvation in the age of the decline of the law. Honen proposed the easy means of salvation available to all: rebirth in Amida's Pure Land by means of invoking Amida's name. Honen acknowledged that all men were so wicked that they could never win their own salvation, even if they followed the holy path perfectly. They would be much better off to realize their imperfection and throw themselves upon the mercy of Amida. In other words, salvation is effected not by man but by the "other power" of Amida.

Sometimes this notion of salvation has been compared to Protestantism in Christianity. There seems to be a common emphasis on the wickedness (or sinfulness) of man, absolute faith in a saving divinity, and salvation definitely effected by the divinity rather than man. While there is some foundation for such comparisons, we should not forget that there is great disparity between Buddhist and Christian concepts. For example, the Buddhist concepts of evil, devotion, and salvation (enlightenment) should not be equated with Protestant Christian teachings of sin, faith, and redemption. As a matter of fact, it would even be difficult for all Protestants to agree on what they mean by sin and faith. It is to be expected that the Amidists, too, would differ on whether good works were unimportant for devotion, or whether they were presupposed as a necessity for reciting the *nembutsu.* Another source of disagreement was whether a person was saved absolutely by just one recitation of the *nembutsu,* or whether one's salvation depended upon constant repetition of the *nembutsu.*

Several priests following Honen elaborated different themes of Pure Land teaching, but did not found separate sects. An exception is Shinran (1173–1263), who rivals Honen in Pure Land history and set up his own Amidist sect, called the Jodo Shin sect. Shinran, too, received his Buddhist training at Hieizan, but became converted to Honen's teaching of faith in Amida. Shinran was even more zealous than Honen in propagating Amidism. Shinran said that the all-important thing was faith in Amida. With his emphasis on the importance of *faith* in Amida, Shinran tended to de-emphasize repetition of Amida's name. He maintained that even "one calling" on the name of Amida was sufficient for salvation, although this notion had been rejected by Honen. (this latter phrase is questional

In every aspect Shinran turned Honen's teaching to the extreme of absolute trust in Amida, completely depreciating man's ability to work his own salvation.

Honen had said, "Even a bad man will be received in Buddha's Land, how much more a good man." However, Shinran placed such trust in Amida and such distrust in man's goodness that he turned this saying around: "Even a good man will be received in Buddha's Land, how much more a bad man."[1] Shinran's emphasis on faith in Amida alone led his followers to reject other Buddhist divinities and especially Shinto divinities *(kami)*. Families belonging to the Jodo Shin sect were exceptional in that their homes featured only the Buddhist altar *(butsudan)* and excluded the customary Shinto altar *(kamidana)*. The followers of Honen became the Jodo (Pure Land) sect, while the followers of Shinran became the Jodo Shinshu (True Pure Land sect), which is usually known by its abbreviated name Shinshu (True sect).

In general, Amidism is one of the most pervasive of all religious movements within Japanese history, the Shinshu being the largest single Buddhist sect. Shinran's importance, at least traditionally, is not limited to his status as a founder. There is a tradition that Shinran was contemptuous of the celibate life of a monk, since such a life presupposed one's own power to attain salvation, and, furthermore, the monastic life implied a lack of faith in the Buddha's grace which could erase all imperfection. Shinran wanted to show that the Buddhist life could be practiced by even the ordinary householder, so he married and raised a family. One account says that Honen himself arranged the marriage. Whether or not this story can be verified, Shinran is popularly venerated as establishing the precedent for a married priesthood. In later times all the Buddhist sects fell into the pattern of a married priesthood. This is a distinctive feature of Japanese Buddhism, one which sets it off from the Buddhism of countries such as Ceylon and Burma, where Theravada Buddhism adheres to a celibate monasticism.

Faith in Amida preceded the founding of the Pure Land sects, and also overflowed the boundaries of these sects. The *nembutsu* was something which the people accepted and practiced regardless of their own temple affiliation. Amida was responsive to all who called on the name of Amida, and all people looked up to Amida as a help in time of need. It is told that on the medieval battlefields the dying warriors sent up their loud pleas for Amida to take them to the Pure Land of Amida. This is just one illustration of how Amidism spread to all groups of people and made Buddhism available to everyone. The Pure Land priests were active both in spreading Buddhist faith in the heart of the cities and in building temples in rural areas.

Nichiren: Faith in the Lotus Sutra as the Exclusive National Buddhism

Nichiren (1222–1282) is one of the most forceful personalities in Japanese history. By his opponents he was bitterly despised; by his followers he was highly emulated. Nichiren began his career, as did most eminent Buddhists of his time, at Hieizan. However, Nichiren's religious experience at Hieizan was radically differ-

---

[1]Masaharu Anesaki, *History of Japanese Religion,* pp. 182–83.

ent from that of his contemporaries, prescribing for him a divergent religious career. At an early age he became convinced that the Lotus Sutra contained the essence of the historical Buddha's teachings. Eventually he conceived of himself as the reformer who alone recognized the true teaching of Tendai and its founder Dengyo Daishi, at a time when other religious currents were dominant. In fact, "Nichiren called himself the reincarnation of the Bodhisattva Jogyo to whom the Lotus Sutra had been entrusted."[2] In his critique of the existing schools and in his reinterpretation of the Lotus Sutra, he actually founded a new, powerful sect.

Several passages in the Lotus Sutra make the claim that the Lotus Sutra is the one true channel of Buddhism. Nichiren accepted this theme in establishing the Lotus Sutra as his basis of inspiration and actual object of veneration. Nichiren interpreted all the turmoils of the times and the very age of the decline of the law as a falling away from the true teaching of the Lotus Sutra. For one thing, this famous scripture teaches that the Buddha is revealed in three bodies: the historical Buddha (Shakyamuni), the cosmic or universal Buddha, and the Buddha of bliss which appears in various forms.

Nichiren used this understanding of the Buddha's concept to criticize the central doctrines of both Shingon and Amidism as fragmentary. The Vairocana Buddha of Shingon is only an expression of the cosmic Buddha; Amida Buddha is only a manifestation of the Buddha of bliss. Nichiren thought that these doctrines neglected the historical Buddha and overlooked the threefold character of the Buddha. His religious convictions also clashed with the other sects on the basic issues of the true object of worship and the true goal of religious life. Nichiren ridiculed the esoterism and ritualism of Shingon as superstitious folly. He was especially critical of Shingon ritualism because it had invaded Hieizan and overshadowed the original Tendai teaching.

Nichiren criticized Amidism for several reasons. In the first place, he objected to the cult of faith in Amida Buddha and repetition of the *nembutsu*. This was not simply a doctrinal criticism, for Nichiren said the true object of worship was the Lotus Sutra itself! Later he composed a graphic representation, or *mandala* (magical picture), of the title of this sutra, which became a primary object of worship. Therefore, he encouraged his followers to venerate and praise this scripture with the phrase "namu Myoho Renge Kyo" (praise to or faith in the wonderful Lotus Sutra). In other words, Nichiren did not really object to the principle of gaining religious power from magical pictures *(mandala)* or from devotional recitation. His real objection was that Shingon and Amida Buddhism did not recognize the proper object of devotion, which was the Lotus Sutra and the recitation of faith in the Lotus Sutra.

Nichiren was also contemptuous of the Pure Land stress on absolute trust in Amida at the expense of human initiative. Nichiren was just as convinced as the Amidists about the decline of the law, but he reacted in a different way. He emphasized the active responsibility of every person to change this decadent

[2]Hajime Nakamura, *Ways of Thinking of Eastern Peoples,* p. 451.

situation, by return to faith in the Lotus Sutra. Some other Buddhist priests thought the disturbed times and corrupt Buddhism could be corrected by a return to the proper monastic rules—a revival of the Ritsu (Vinaya) expression of Buddhism. Nichiren dismissed this movement, too, since he measured everything in terms of the Lotus Sutra. At the same time Zen was becoming a major factor in Japanese Buddhism. Nichiren had no use for the Zen form of Buddhist meditation.

Nichiren's uncompromising character is evident in his unbending criticism of the other contemporary Buddhist groups, but this trait is even more strongly accentuated in the founding of his own movement. For example, in Japan, religion and country have always been closely associated. Nichiren did not stop with criticism of other sects; he went so far as to say that the religion of the Lotus Sutra should be adopted as the state religion and all other Buddhist sects should be annihilated. This is perhaps the most extreme expression of the typical Japanese association of religion and nation (or political state). In fact, Nichiren was as much a patriot as a religious leader. His whole life can be seen as a valiant attempt to save Japan, making use of the teachings of the Lotus Sutra. He suffered severe persecution for his outspokenness, several times narrowly escaping execution. But he thought little of this, since it was in the service of Buddhism and his country. He is well remembered for having made the prediction that the Mongols would attempt to invade Japan, a prediction which came true within his lifetime. The Mongol invasion was interpreted by Nichiren as a combination of punishment for Japan's (Japanese Buddhism's) evils, and a sign of the age of the decline of the law.[3]

Although the Nichiren sect is not the largest of Buddhist groups, it has been one of the most active. Not every Nichiren follower had the sense of mission of the founder, but this peculiar development has great significance for later history. It fed into nationalistic streams before World War II, and also helped spawn important New Religions such as Soka Gakkai, all of which focus on the Lotus Sutra. Nichiren Buddhism can be seen both as an authentic Japanese Buddhism and as a Buddhism of the Japanese people.

The Zen Sects: Enlightenment for the Military and Refinement for the Arts

Zen is certainly the most publicized, but not necessarily the most understood, aspect of Japanese Buddhism. Due to the great Western interest in Zen, many Westerners have been led to believe that Zen tells the whole story of Japanese Buddhism and the Japanese spirit. In this short work the treatment of Zen must be limited to its role within Japanese religious history. There is already a vast

---

[3]The Mongol fleet was destroyed by a storm which the Shinto proponents chose to interpret as a "divine wind" *(kamikaze)*. Thus, the Shinto interpretation stressed that native gods had driven out the foreigners. In World War II the airplanes of the suicide pilots who crashed their planes into Allied ships were also called *kamikaze*.

popular literature for Westerners dealing with contemporary Zen as a personal philosophy of life, to which the reader may refer. However, to understand Zen historically, we must recognize that in Japan it first rose to prominence during the Kamakura period. Therefore, it shared the same religious and cultural atmosphere as Pure Land and Nichiren Buddhism.

Zen cannot be divorced from its Indian and Chinese origins. As one Japanese scholar has described the problem, "Zen combined with the intellectual culture of India, the pragmatic culture of China, and the esthetic culture of Japan."[4] The word Zen derives from the Sanskrit word *dhyana,* meaning meditation. However, the practice of meditation did not form the basis of a separate school until this stream had entered China, where it became related to Taoistic conceptions and practice of Taoism. The Chinese sects of Ch'an (Chinese for *dhyana*) formed the basis for the Japanese sects of Zen (the Japanese pronunciation of Ch'an).

Zen was known in Japan several centuries before Kamakura times, without becoming a major movement. Several of the earlier priests who went to China on imperial order brought back Zen. Dengyo Daishi, the founder of Tendai, visited Zen Monasteries in China and brought back the Zen practices of meditation. Nevertheless, Zen at Hieizan could not hold its own against Dengyo Daishi's teaching of the Lotus Sutra, the dominant Shingon esoterism which overshadowed Heian times, and the emerging Amidist beliefs. In effect, Zen had to be reimported by forceful personalities who made a special effort to propagate Zen. The two most important figures are Eisai (1141–1215) and Dogen (1200–1253).

Eisai received a thorough training in Buddhism at Hieizan, but still was not satisfied with the contemporary forms of Buddhism. He wanted to go to India to search out the true Buddhism, but actually traveled only as far as China, making two trips there. In China he was converted to the Lin-chi sect of Ch'an (Zen) Buddhism and received the full training of this sect. His return to Japan marks the beginning of the Japanese Zen sect of Rinzai. (Rinzai is the Japanese pronunciation for Lin-chi.) There is a tradition that he was responsible for the introduction of tea into Japan. Eisai had little luck in advocating Zen around the capital city of Kyoto, where the older sects were still entrenched. However, he found continuing support from the military warlords at Kamakura.

In China, too, Zen (Ch'an) had been partly a reaction against the scholasticism and formalism found in some imported forms of Indian Buddhism. In place of innumerable abstract doctrines, the Zen devotees set forth a simple notion that every person could attain enlightenment by insight into his own experience and the world around him. The Lin-chi (Rinzai) sect placed emphasis on a sudden enlightenment which might be triggered by an accidental circumstance which enlightened the person about the true nature of himself and the world. It is only natural that Zen would make a good showing in the Kamakura age when Buddhism was appealing to the masses in simpler terms. Whereas the Amida cults stressed faith in Amida and Nichiren advocated faith in the Lotus Sutra, the Zen

---

[4]Reiho Masunaga, *The Soto Approach to Zen,* p. 34.

II. DEVELOPMENT AND ELABORATION

priests replaced complicated doctrines with a notion of immediate enlightenment in one's everyday life. It is no wonder that the military leaders of Kamakura would find appealing this notion of the sudden, incisive enlightenment. On the other hand, Eisai had to make certain compromises to the military rulers and to established Buddhists in order to have Zen recognized as a separate sect.

Dogen (1200–1253) is supposed to have met Eisai before the latter's death. Dogen went to see Eisai after being disappointed in his studies of Buddhism at Hieizan. After Eisai's death Dogen went to China, but still could not gain satisfaction in the Buddhist teachings there. Finally he attained enlightenment under the guidance of a Zen master and received the training of the Ts'ao-tung sect. He returned to Japan to spread this new-found version of Zen. (Ts'ao-tung is pronounced Soto in Japanese.) However, Dogen was more uncompromising than Eisai and could not bring himself to serve the military rulers. This made his life all the more difficult, but later his Soto sect of Zen flourished.

The difference between Rinzai Zen and Soto Zen is roughly the same in China and Japan. Rinzai favors the use of such techniques as *koan*, comparable to riddles, contemplation on which leads to enlightenment. The Soto sect, which was introduced by Dogen, gives some weight to study of the scriptures, and emphasizes the gradual entry into enlightenment. The Soto sect is famous for its practice of *zazen*, "sitting in meditation." However, in contrast with the Chinese Ts'ao-tung sect of Zen, because of Dogen's two emphases "on scriptural authority and on faith in Buddha . . . the Soto Zen school in Japan was Dogen's unique creation."[5]

It would be misleading to treat Zen only in terms of its doctrinal developments. It is true that Zen has its roots in India, emerged as a sect in China, and first flourished in Japan as the imported Rinzai and Soto sects. But Zen is much more than a sect expression of Buddhism or a personal experience of enlightenment. In both China and Japan, Zen made an overwhelming impact on the arts. While Shingon had made some contribution to the graphic arts, Zen pervaded the whole culture. Zen (colored by Taoism's love of nature) is the spiritual resource for much of Chinese and Japanese painting, and can be seen even in the more mundane art of flower arranging *(ikebana).* Shingon art favors the esoteric and even borders on the grotesque, but Zen favors a quiet simplicity.

It is difficult to say whether the Chinese tradition of Ch'an (Zen) taught quiet simplicity to the Japanese, or whether the Japanese brought a cultural tradition of quiet simplicity to their understanding of Zen. However, from ancient times the Japanese have had a peculiar tradition combining aesthetic and religious appreciation of nature. This can be seen as early as the pioneer anthology of poetry, the *Manyoshu.* Many Westerners have come to appreciate Zen through translations of the short, "telegraphic" poems called *haiku* which express the spirit of Zen. Also, the drinking of tea and the cult of tea has been closely associated with Zen.

---

[5]Joseph M. Kitagawa, *Religion in Japanese History,* p. 129.

10. Elaboration Within Japanese Buddhism   *67*

Zen has pervaded Japanese culture even beyond the realms of what Westerners ordinarily understand as art. Zen practitioners cared less for subtlety of doctrine than they cared for the complete training of mind and body. There was a relationship between emphasis on the instant of enlightenment, and having mind and body tuned to every instant of experience. Therefore, military techniques or sports such as swordsmanship, archery, and wrestling were pursued for the sake of Zen. The object was not simply to defeat the opponent, but to tune one's whole person to a naturalness and freeness which escaped the formalities of prescribed movements. It is no wonder that the Kamakura warriors adopted Zen, both for its utilitarian and spiritual benefits. In the modern period Zen continues to be a major inspiration for philosophical thought and religious cultivation.

In order to understand the development and elaboration of Buddhism it has been necessary to point out the new waves of Buddhism and the peculiar doctrinal developments. However, this does not mean that the Japanese people who accepted Buddhism were completely aware of all these points of doctrine. Buddhism made its impression on Japanese life in a more direct fashion. We must not forget, amidst these discussions of doctrine, that Japanese Buddhism has always been important for carrying out the indispensable memorials for family ancestors. Even Nichiren, seen by some as a religious fanatic and superpatriot, is said to have spent much time in prayer for the departed souls of his parents and teacher. One way of viewing the sect developments is to recognize that they set up special channels within which these practical functions could be carried out. In addition to the memorial services, temples held regular festivals and issued various protective charms. The people who had memorial services performed at the temple or went there for other reasons might not be closely acquainted with the peculiar doctrines of that sect.

SELECTED READINGS

Anesaki, Masaharu. *Nichiren the Buddhist Prophet.* An earlier publication, but still the standard biography of Nichiren in English.
Bloom, Alfred. *Shinran's Gospel of Pure Grace.* A concise study of Shinran's thought.
Coates, Harper Havelock, and Ishizuka, Ryugaku. *Honen the Buddhist Saint. His Life and Teaching.* A careful study of Honen.
Dumoulin, Heinrich. *A History of Zen Buddhism.* The best historical treatment of Zen; includes a convenient bibliography.
Earhart, H. Byron. *Religion in the Japanese Experience.* See pp. 131–44 and 197–200 for materials related to Zen.
Kapleau, Philip. *The Three Pillars of Zen. Teaching, Practice, and Enlightenment.* Interprets the nature of Zen practice and its significance for modern man.
Sansom, Sir George. *A History of Japan,* Vol. I, pp. 409–37. Provides a general picture of the Kamakura period, including an overview of "Religious Trends."
Suzuki, D.T. *Zen and Japanese Culture.* Describes the Zen penetration of Japanese culture.
Tsunoda, Ryusaku, *et al. Sources of Japanese Tradition.* See Chapter 10 for translated documents concerning the Pure Land sects, Chapter 11 for translated documents

concerning the Nichiren sect, and Chapter 12 for translated documents concerning the Zen sect.

11.

The Development of Medieval Shinto

Medieval Buddhism and Medieval Shinto

In Chapter 3 we saw how Shinto became organized partly in reaction to the influx of continental traditions such as Buddhism. In later chapters we discussed the development of Buddhism, Confucianism, and religious Taoism within Japanese history. Chapters 9 and 10 demonstrated the amazing amount of vitality and innovation within Japanese Buddhism of the ninth through the thirteenth centuries. It may seem that Shinto has been crowded out of the historical picture by the attempt to discuss foreign importations such as Buddhism. As a matter of fact, Shinto was overshadowed by the flourishing of Buddhism. Most of the emperors and the nobility favored Buddhism, and the court was mainly concerned with Buddhism. Thus, if we look at the capital and the formal organization of the state, Buddhism seems to have completely conquered the native religion. Of course, Buddhism's domination was not complete, because even at the capital Shinto lived on in the state cult headed by the emperor.

However, the "great tradition" which dominated the political and literary life is only one side of Japanese religious history. There is also the "little tradition" which expressed the cultural and religious life of the people.[1] The common people outside of the capital lived their religious lives primarily in terms of annual festivals connected with agriculture and other vocations. Many shrines and festivals existed before the entry of Buddhism and continued naturally with or without the influence of Buddhism. While Buddhism dominated the court, Shinto with its loosely organized religious life centering on local shrines remained the prevailing religion of the countryside.

Buddhism never completely superseded Shinto. In fact, as long as Buddhism was centered at the capital, it tended to remain the religion of the aristocracy. Nara Buddhism made very little impact on the people. Even the Tendai and Shingon sects of Heian Buddhism, with the express purpose of developing a Japanese Buddhism, fell short of their goal. Buddhism could become a religion of the people only when it entered the life of the people. In part, Shinto's appropriation of Buddhist systems helped Buddhism make its appeal to the people. Even-

---

[1] For an application of Robert Redfield's notions of little tradition and great tradition to an example of Japanese religious history, see Ichiro Hori, *Folk Religion in Japan*, pp. 49–81; an excerpt from Hori's work is included in H. Byron Earhart, *Religion in the Japanese Experience*, pp. 193–97.

II. DEVELOPMENT AND ELABORATION

tually the people accepted the various Buddhist *bodhisattvas* on the same level as their Japanese *kami*. Therefore, although Buddhism seemed to triumph on the surface, the religious life of Shinto persevered—even within the Buddhist forms. Neither Buddhism nor Shinto can be considered the victor in this process of mutual adaptation. While Buddhism was being transformed into a Japanese movement, Shinto was quietly incorporating the various strands of continental influence.

Borrowing by Medieval Shinto

The development of medieval Shinto is the result of more than a simple encounter with Buddhism. In the Heian and Kamakura periods, when Chinese culture was so highly esteemed, Shinto tended to draw into itself elements of Confucianism, religious Taoism, and Buddhism—especially speculative philosophy and cosmology from Buddhism. In general, Shinto borrowed various kinds of religious expressions from the three traditions. Ethical concepts came from Confucianism; religious Taoism provided cosmology, a religious calendar, divinities, festivals, and charms; Buddhism furnished philosophy, cosmology, rituals, objects of worship, and formulas.

Shinto's practice of borrowing must be seen from two viewpoints in order to understand it. On the one hand, Shinto never ceased to be the perpetuator of the older Japanese traditions, and usually borrowed foreign concepts in order to complement or explain Shinto traditions. In this sense, Shinto did remain Shinto in spite of the borrowings. On the other hand, these borrowings became so much a part of Shinto that eventually their foreign character was forgotten. In this sense, the already complex character of Shinto became much more complex, such that it cannot be called simply the indigenous religion of Japan. These borrowed traditions added to the richness of Shinto and enabled it to become more systematically organized.

"Medieval Shinto" is an approximate term which refers to Shinto when it was actively borrowing from other traditions and organizing itself on borrowed patterns, especially from about the twelfth through the sixteenth centuries. However, the outside limits of medieval Shinto are difficult to set, since Shinto never was a completely isolated tradition. The precedent for Shinto's borrowing from other traditions was already established in the Nara period, but perhaps it may be said that medieval Shinto took shape and flourished from the Heian period onward. The terminal date for medieval Shinto is officially 1868, the date of the Meiji Restoration, when Shinto and Buddhism were forcibly separated. Shinto purists had been working for this separation for several centuries before 1868.

Perhaps the best way to introduce the complicated phenomenon of medieval Shinto is to discuss it in terms of the traditions which influenced it. Although Buddhism was not the only influential tradition, it was undoubtedly the most influential. For example, one Buddhist theory pervaded practically the whole of Shinto, apart from specific influences of Buddhist sects. This is the Buddhist theory of *honji-suijaku* ("original substance manifests traces"). In brief, it is the theoretical foundation for considering Japanese *kami* as the "manifest traces" (*suijaku*) of the "original substance" (*honji*) of particular Buddhas and *bodhisattvas.* Already in the Nara period Hachiman was considered both as a *kami* for Shinto and a *bodhisattva* for Buddhism. In later periods almost every Shinto shrine considered its enshrined *kami* as the counterpart of some Buddha or Buddhist divinity. It was customary to enshrine statues of these Buddhist counterparts in Shinto shrines, and this further encouraged the interaction of Buddhist and Shinto priests. It should be noted that the mixture of Buddhism with local Japanese religion is not unique in the history of Buddhism. The Buddhist pantheon had been closely associated with other divinities in India, and then in China it developed counterparts of various Chinese deities.

One reason why medieval Shinto is difficult to outline is the fact that it was never uniformly systematized. For example, the theory of *honji-suijaku* was put into practice in many local shrines throughout the country, but there was no uniform set of counterparts for Shinto *kami* and Buddhist divinities. Shinto shrines might be dedicated to the worship of divinities either Buddhist, Chinese, or even Indian in origin. Shinto priests (and Buddhist priests and the people) could participate religiously in this ambiguous context without making any precise relationships or sharp distinctions. We have seen that this undefined sense of harmony among the several religious traditions is a persistent theme throughout Japanese religious history.

We remember that when the Way of Buddha (Butsudo) entered Japan it stimulated the formation of the Way of *Kami* (Shinto). Thereafter Buddhism and Shinto were in informal contact with one another; but it was not until the Heian period that the Tendai and Shingon sects openly favored cooperation between Buddhism and Shinto. Medieval Shinto arose in the Heian period and borrowed from the Tendai and Shingon sects for two main reasons. First, these two Buddhist sects actively assumed a Japanese character, making them acceptable to Shinto; second, both sects possessed the richer cosmology, philosophy, and ritual which Shinto apparently desired. There were earlier precedents of Shinto-Buddhist cooperation, which Shinto scholars could use in the Heian period to borrow heavily from Tendai and Shingon in building up a more glorious Shinto system.

The Relation of Tendai and Shingon to Medieval Shinto

The first elaborate system of borrowing between Shinto and Buddhism was at Hieizan, the mountain headquarters of Tendai. To a certain extent the basic mode of borrowing was similar at Koyasan, the mountain headquarters of Shingon. At this time Shinto shrines and Buddhist temples stood side by side, with some mutual participation by priests of Shinto and Buddhism. The founders of the two Buddhist sects, Dengyo Daishi and Kobo Daishi, thought it only natural that shrines should be erected to honor the local *kami* of their respective mountains. Gradually there arose at each locale individual forms of thought and practice that related the Shinto *kami* and Buddhist doctrine. Since the Tendai headquarters was modeled after the Chinese mountain headquarters by the same name (T'ien-t'ai in Chinese), the Tendai scholars had a precedent to follow in recognizing the local deity. The name for the local deity, adopted from the Chinese, was "mountain king" (pronounced Sanno in Japanese). The theoretical foundation of the system, according to Tendai, was found in its highly revered Lotus Sutra. In this text is a statement that all the Buddhas which come into the world are only "one reality" (*ichi jitsu*)—the Tendai concept of an absolute reality behind the whole universe. The theory was used to argue that the various *kami* are Japanese historical appearances which correspond to Buddhist divinities, all of which are subsumed in the "one reality." This form of Shinto was called either Sanno Shinto or Ichi-jitsu Shinto. While this brief presentation may have given the impression that borrowing was mainly intellectual, the contrary is true: at a popular level, there was a ritual and devotional union of Shinto and Buddhism. Officially Shinto was separated from Buddhism after 1868, but even today Sanno shrines survive. Although explicit Buddhist influence has been removed from the shrines, the very existence of Sanno shrines is a continuing reminder of the earlier Shinto-Buddhist intermixture.

In the same vein, we can see Shinto absorbing the Shingon notion that the whole world can best be understood through two *mandalas* (world pictures). These symbolic pictures of the cosmos represented the bipolar character of existence witnessed in such things as matter-mind, male-female, diamond-womb, or dynamic expression-static potential. With this ideological framework Shinto priests could coordinate Japanese *kami* and Buddhist divinities; for they could place some *kami* within the womb *mandala*, other *kami* within the diamond *mandala*. Because this syncretistic style of Shinto emphasized the two *mandala* of Shingon, it was called Ryobu Shinto. *Ryobu* means two parts or dual, and sometimes Ryobu Shinto has been translated as "Dual Shinto." A famous example of the rationale of Ryobu Shinto is found at the Ise shrines, the most venerated shrines in Japan. Amaterasu, the Sun Goddess and ancestress of the imperial family, is enshrined at Ise. In later times the Sun Goddess came to be equated with the Sun Buddha of the *Mahavairocana Sutra*, which is the main scripture of Shingon. The Ise Shrines, which include the Inner Shrine and Outer Shrine, came to be considered as the representation of the two *mandala* of Shingon.

As in the case of Shinto's incorporation of Tendai Buddhist elements, Shinto borrowed Shingon ritual, such as the fire rite, and even architectural forms, together with theoretical elements. A shrine which received the influence of Ryobu Shinto can be identified even today by the peculiar *torii* (sacred arch) in front of it. There are various kinds of Shinto *torii*, all of which feature two upright poles with a crosspiece connecting the poles. In Ryobu Shinto the *torii* was modified so that each upright pole had attached to it two smaller poles. The two smaller poles indicate the dual character of the world which is transcended by an overarching unity.

11. The Development of Medieval Shinto   73

The Development of Medieval Shinto

Tendai and Shingon influenced Shinto most strongly where their temples stood near shrines. However, the interpenetration experienced by some Buddhist and Shinto centers is not the whole story. Medieval Shinto can be said to have developed in at least two other manners. One was through the traditions maintained by hereditary Shinto priestly families. Another was through individual Shinto scholars. For example, the Japanese tradition of religious Taoism (Onmyodo) entered medieval Shinto through the Shinto families who had carried on the traditions formerly within the government bureau of divination. Naturally, this school emphasized the important role of divination. Even outside these hereditary families, the *yin-yang* notion of religious Taoism was already available as early as the writing of the *Nihongi*. Medieval Shinto received the influence of religious Taoism from its earliest traces in Japan, both directly from these hereditary families, and indirectly from the Taoistic traditions incorporated within Shingon. The charms and divinities of religious Taoism penetrated both Buddhism and Shinto. Confucianism was an indirect influence on Shinto thinkers, since their education was still heavily Confucian.[2]

From the very moment when Shinto arose, we see a general picture of Shinto appropriating as much as it could of the continental traditions. Shinto was not a passive recipient of these influences; rather, Shinto was actively adapting the new elements. The reason for this appropriation and adaptation was to strengthen and organize Shinto more effectively. As Shinto became more self-confident, it attempted once more to assert its distinctiveness and superiority.

The best example of Shinto adaptation is the Yui-itsu (or Yui-ichi) school of Shinto. This movement reversed the former interpretation of *honji-suijaku* so that the Japanese *kami* was regarded as the "original substance" (*honji*) and the Buddhist divinity as the "manifest trace" (*suijaku*), giving the superior position to the Japanese *kami*. The Yui-itsu school of Shinto, sometimes named after the Yoshida or Urabe family, developed a comprehensive pantheistic system on this basic principle, making Shinto into an all-embracing philosophy and religion. The Yui-itsu school and other Shinto scholars used similar schemes to try to set themselves apart from Buddhism, Confucianism, and Taoism. However, from our historical vantage point we can see that they could not escape from their borrowed influence. Such pantheistic schemes demonstrated the very Buddhist influence they were trying to escape. Nevertheless, these movements are important for understanding the growing Shinto concern to "purify" itself and to regain its former position of glory.

A long line of writers from medieval times onward supported the cause of a purified Shinto. The most famous of the early writers is Kitabatake Chikafusa

---

[2]Much later, in the nineteenth century, several Shinto sects were formed around Confucian doctrines.

(1293–1354), who supported the divine descent of the imperial line and argued for the superiority of Shinto over the foreign traditions. A more systematic writer, the foremost proponent of Yui-itsu Shinto, is Yoshida Kanetomo (1435–1511). One Japanese scholar of Shinto has written, "From this inexhaustible intellectual fountain-head of Kanetomo's theology almost every later Shinto theological school of the Tokugawa period takes its source. . . ."[3] Kanetomo depended heavily on a thirteenth-century writing of the Ise priests, called *Gobusho*. The *Gobusho*, a collection of five writings, and sometimes described as the Shinto Pentateuch, is a good example of how Shinto became organized partly in reaction to Buddhism. Shinto writers composed the *Gobusho* so that they, too, would have a scripture. The writing drew heavily on foreign themes.

A number of nebulous Shinto schools formed themselves around one or more of these borrowed traditions. But they remained schools—lines of teaching—and did not become separate sects until about the nineteenth century. The Shinto schools never had the distinct existence that Buddhist sects enjoyed. Perhaps this is a significant clue to medieval Shinto. Shinto possessed unique Japanese traditions which were very important for the life of the country—and yet Shinto lacked a glorious system by which to express these traditions. Shinto lacked the philosophical subtlety and completeness which Buddhism possessed. The motive for Shinto's borrowing was not to create a tradition, but to elaborate the Shinto tradition into a full-blown system equal to any foreign tradition.

We must never forget the vitality and broad base of Shinto. As early as 927 the Institutes of the Engi period (*Engishiki*) recorded more than 6,000 Shinto shrines where annual offerings were made by officials of the court or provincial government.[4] This was a big step in organizing and ranking the loosely affiliated shrines. Gradually local shrines became more closely related to the regional community and more directly related to the formal Shinto pantheon. Although many early shrines were practically the possession of individual clans and their blood relations, eventually these shrines became the place of worship for all the people of that area. This set the pattern for the traditional village shrine with the village (or village sub-divisions) as the geographical parish. During medieval times when powerful clans began to open up the northern part of Japan, they established branch shrines of their famous clan shrines in their new homes in northern Japan. These branch shrines, too, became important regional worship centers for the surrounding people. At the same time there was a tendency for Shinto scholars to insist that the object of worship in local shrines had to corre-

[3]Genchi Kato, "The Theological System of Urabe no Kanetomo," pp. 149–50. (Yoshida and Urabe refer to the same family line; it is customary to refer to such famous scholars by their given names. In the text of this book all Japanese names follow the Japanese practice of giving the family name first.)

[4]See Ryusaku Tsunoda, *et al., Sources of Japanese Tradition*, Chapter 13. For a translation of Books I–V of the *Engishiki*, see Felicia Gressitt Bock, *Engi-shiki*.

11. The Development of Medieval Shinto

spond to one of the *kami* in the *Kojiki* or *Nihongi*. Although these *kami* were specified as the official objects of worship at local shrines, this change did not really alter the rituals at the shrines and the faith of the worshipers.

The true power of the shrines system is seen in the times leading up to World War II, when Shinto became the chief mechanism of the state for inculcating patriotism under the guise of venerating the emperor. Throughout the middle ages political power rested almost completely in the hands of the military rulers, but the emperor was still held in high regard by the people and at least respected by the military rulers. The emperor had an important role in continuing Shinto ceremonies on behalf of the nation. At the same time, the emperors were deeply concerned with Buddhism and it was often the custom for the emperor to abdicate after a short reign, becoming a Buddhist monk.[5]

SELECTED READINGS

Holtom, Daniel C. *The National Faith of Japan*. See pp. 30–52 for a historical treatment of the transition from early to medieval Shinto.

Kato, Genchi. "The Theological System of Urabe no Kanetomo." Treats the general significance of the medieval Shinto theologian, Kanetomo.

Matsunaga, Alicia. *The Buddhist Philosophy of Assimilation*. Provides an interpretation of the "unification of gods and Buddhas" from the viewpoint of Buddhism; see Earhart, *Religion in the Japanese Experience*, pp. 39–44 for excerpts from Matsunaga.

Tsunoda, Ryusaku, *et al. Sources of Japanese Tradition*. See Chapter 13 for an introduction to medieval Shinto, with translated documents.

---

[5]For a fascinating excerpt from a fourteenth century emperor's diary, and other religious aspects of the medieval age, see Sir George Sansom, *A History of Japan*, Vol. II, pp. 127–40.

12.

The Appearance of Christianity in Japan

Christianity: A New Tradition in Japanese Religious History

By the middle of the sixteenth century all the basic traditions within Japanese religion had interacted to a great degree and also developed distinctive lines of transmission. In 1549 Christianity was introduced into the Japanese islands by Roman Catholic missionaries. The Japanese, being rather self-conscious of their own distinctive blend of various traditions into a Japanese culture, did not at first understand Christianity, but viewed it as a foreign religion. Christianity was one of several European cultural influences to which the Japanese reacted during the sixteenth century. It may be argued that Christianity did not become transformed into a Japanese religion, as had happened with Buddhism. Nevertheless, an examination of "The Christian Century in Japan," as one scholar has described it, gives us many insights into Japanese religious history.

The first Christian missionary to Japan was Saint Francis Xavier, later called the Apostle of Japan. Xavier was drawn to Japan by favorable accounts of this wonderful country, and his first impression verified these rumors. In a few years he saw an encouraging number of converts and foresaw a glorious future for the Roman church. He did not underestimate the faith of the most sincere converts, but neither did he suspect the great trials to which their faith would be subjected. Within a century's time the foreign priests and Japanese Christians experienced a persecution which some scholars say is unparalleled in the history of the Christian church. By about 1650 Christianity ceased to exist as a public religion, surviving only on a small scale as a secret cult. This brief episode of church history in sixteenth- and seventeenth-century Japan forms an interesting aspect of Japanese religious history.

The Success of Christianity as a Foreign Religion

The motives for missionary work, both Christian and Buddhist, have usually included a mixture of religious, economic, and cultural factors. The entry of Christianity into sixteenth-century Japan was no exception. The earliest missionaries were chiefly Portuguese Jesuits, and the same ships which brought the Jesuits carried European goods for trade. The economic support of the Jesuits was closely related to this trade, and it was no secret that the Japanese feudal lords desired the presence of a Jesuit priest in order to attract trade with the Portuguese ships.

Xavier at first traveled to the capital with the purpose of speaking to the "king" of Japan; he found out that in the mid-sixteenth century the emperor was only a figurehead, since real political power was held by a military ruler and local feudal lords. The Jesuits learned that without the cooperation—or at least the tolerance—of the feudal lords, they could do nothing. A feudal lord often would declare for Christianity more or less superficially, and his subjects would follow suit. The Jesuits were well aware of the expediency of these conversions, but accepted the situation because at least it enabled them to work for genuine converts.

Xavier left Japan reluctantly after two years of work, but a handful of priests remained to carry on the work. Gradually other Roman Catholic orders were represented, but there never was a great number of priests in Japan. (The unfriendly rivalry betwen Jesuits and other Catholic orders constituted a major obstacle to effective missionary work, and also may have made the military rulers suspicious of all foreigners.) However, there was an increasing number of conversions, and the attraction to Christianity cannot be explained simply in economic terms. In accounting for these conversions to Christianity we can understand something about the nature of Christianity itself, the contemporary religious scene in Japan, and the Japanese people.

Christianity offered an unambiguous and uncompromising picture of salvation. At first some basic Christian doctrines, such as a Creator God and sin, seemed incomprehensible, but once the Japanese understood, many became unswerving believers. This is not surprising, especially in view of the Buddhist sects which had appeared since Heian times—the Pure Land sects, Zen, and Nichiren. Each of them stressed an assurance of salvation in a distinctive fashion. Christianity offered assurance of salvation in its own distinctive fashion. This does not mean that Roman Catholicism was mistaken for a Buddhist development, but it does help provide a context for understanding how the Japanese people could accept this radically different religious tradition. The contemporary religious scene was pervaded by the increasing decadence of the Buddhist sects. The older sects of Tendai and Shingon, as well as the newer sects of Pure Land, Zen, and Nichiren, were economic and military headquarters, which tended to compromise their religious character. The general decline of the Buddhist sects seems to have been a contributing factor to the success of Christian missions. In fact, it seems that the anti-Buddhist attitude of the military ruler Oda Nobunaga (1534–1582) may have been one reason for his rather friendly relations with the Christian missionaries. An outstanding feature of the Japanese people is their sensitivity to the foreign and exotic. This sensitivity is ambivalent—it can mean wholehearted adoption or complete rejection, but at least the Japanese have always been greatly interested in things foreign. During the heyday of Portuguese influence it was the fad at court to wear Portuguese clothes and to spice one's conversation with Portuguese words. The Christianity of this early period is still remembered by the

II. DEVELOPMENT AND ELABORATION

Japanese term "Kirishitan," a corrupt borrowing of the Portuguese word *Christao*, for Christian. At first Christianity benefited from its status as a foreign religion, whereas later it was persecuted and abolished for the same reason.

The Expulsion of Christianity as a Foreign Religion

The fortunes—and misfortunes—of Roman Catholicism in medieval Japan were closely linked to the careers of three great military leaders and unifiers of Japan. They are Oda Nobunaga (1534–1582), Toyotomi Hideyoshi (1536–1598), and Tokugawa Ieyasu (1542–1616). During Nobunaga's rule Christianity flourished with his consent. It is said that Nobunaga was motivated not so much by his love for Christianity, as by his hatred for Buddhism. Nobunaga, in trying to unify the country politically, saw the large Buddhist headquarters as political and military threats. Several times Nobunaga saw fit to punish the Buddhist strongholds with military force. In 1571, for example, he completely devastated the Tendai mountain of Hieizan, in the process massacring all monks, laymen, and even women and children. It is thought that Nobunaga may have allowed Christianity to grow only with the ulterior motive of having it check the strength of Buddhism.

Nobunaga's successor Hideyoshi turned into a persecutor of the Christian church. The reasons for this change are veiled in the passage of time. The reversal of policy, however, may be connected with a general suspicion that the Catholic fathers really had secret plans to take over Japan. At any rate, Hideyoshi still encouraged trade with the Portuguese while proscribing the Christian faith. In actuality, the Edict against Christianity was not rigorously enforced, and the result was that more converts were added to the church during this period of mild persecution.

Ieyasu, the next ruler, made good the threats of his predecessors by actually driving the foreign missionaries from Japan. Whereas his predecessors had been antagonistic towards Buddhism, Ieyasu's personal life was influenced by Buddhist piety, while his government policy was supported by Confucian ideals. Ieyasu is one of the most imposing figures in all Japanese history. He was so revered that he was deified by his own priestly advisor as the Sun God of the East.[1] An imposing shrine serves as his tomb of enshrinement at Nikko, and branch shrines dedicated to him are found throughout Japan. His decree of 1614 meant the physical deportation of all foreign missionaries and some leading Christians. Although Ieyasu did not shed any blood, his successors provided many martyrs for the church. Priests who had defied the edict to stay in Japan, and the loyal Japanese Christians who hid them, were executed. The most hideous tortures were devised to make these foreign priests and Japanese Christians recant their faith, the purpose being to refute Christianity publicly. The tortures were only

---

[1]See "The Sun God of the East" in Chapter 15, *Sources of Japanese Tradition,* Ryusaku Tsunoda, *et al.* For remarks on this pattern of "immanental theocracy," see Joseph M. Kitagawa, *Religion in Japanese History,* pp. 154, 161.

partially successful in gaining formal renunciation of the faith among the people. Gradually the foreign priests were all hunted down, and later attempts to land missionaries resulted in immediate capture.

One of the decisive events in the downfall of Catholicism was the Shimabara Revolt of 1637–38 by Japanese Christians in Kyushu. Due to the hardships of peasant life and oppressive government policy, many peasants and some warriors occasionally revolted against the government. In fact, Pure Land and Nichiren groups had also become involved in social and economic protest. In the bloody Shimabara Revolt (as with the previous revolts),"The revolt was not primarily a religious uprising, but a desperate protest against the oppressive rule of feudal lords in a remote and backward region."[2] Nevertheless, in this feudal context any rival faith represented a threat to social stability, and the feudal government used the Shimabara Revolt (when many thousands were killed) as a precedent for abolishing Christianity. This led to the exclusion order of 1639 which strictly prohibited any future visits by Portuguese ships on penalty of destruction of ship and crew. In 1640 when a Portuguese ship came to Japan on a diplomatic mission to negotiate this decree, the ship and almost all of the crew were destroyed. By about 1650 Christianity became an underground religion. The Japanese authorities thought they had completely abolished this foreign religion, but in reality it was handed down as a secret tradition within certain families, particularly in the Kyushu region where Christianity had gained its strongest foothold.

The Significance of the Christian Century for Understanding Japanese Religion

It is ironic that Christianity took on a Japanese character only when it was deprived of ordained priests and went underground. Japanese customs and beliefs became naturally mixed with Christian beliefs. Interestingly enough, one of the persistent arguments against Christianity in the edicts was that Christianity was anti-Japanese and against the Japanese religious traditions. Christianity was considered to be anti-Japanese in the sense that a Japanese Christian was loyal to foreign gods and to foreign priests, rather than to native *kami* and to his Japanese feudal lord. Christianity was considered to be contrary to the Japanese religious traditions, since it introduced foreign gods and contradictory doctrines.

Christianity certainly presented a contrast to the general theme in Japanese religion that traditions harmonize with one another rather than making exclusive claims to absolute truth. The Jesuits were very effective in their active policy of acquiring the language and customs of the country, but in matters of religious doctrine and practice they were not so flexible. It is curious that Buddhism, once seen by the Japanese as a foreign religion and for that reason opposed as offensive to the native *kami,* had become thoroughly assimilated within Japanese culture. Although they lost much of their original Indian and Chinese features, both

---

[2]Sir George Sansom, *A History of Japan,* Vol. III, p. 38.

Buddhism and Confucianism were considered as full-fledged Japanese traditions which had the right to oust the foreign Christian religion. By contrast, Christianity has never become Japanized to the extent that it could be considered as a Japanese tradition to oppose foreign traditions.

This brief Christian century in Japan may seem relatively unimportant in the long stretch of Japanese history, but it is very important for understanding later developments. The success of the Catholic missionaries is nothing to gloss over. The number of Catholic priests was always small, never exceeding two hundred, and yet they succeeded in gaining as many as 300,000 converts. (The early missionaries claimed as many as several million converts, but modern scholars such as Boxer and Father Laures adjust this figure to between 200,000 and 300,000 converts.) If the population of Japan during this century was 20,000,000, a higher percentage of the population was Christian at that time than Japan has ever known since. This is rather remarkable in the light of the large numbers of Catholic and Protestant missionaries who have spent great sums of money during the past century with a lower percentage of total Christian converts, Protestant and Catholic combined.

The Christian century in Japan is even more important for influencing later developments in Japanese history. Some scholars feel that the threat of Christianity—real or imagined—was the direct cause of Japan's momentous policy of the closed country which isolated Japan from foreign influence between the mid-seventeenth and mid-nineteenth centuries. Furthermore, in order to stamp out Christianity, every family was required to belong to a Buddhist temple. In effect, this made Buddhism an arm of the government, giving it a great advantage over Shinto. We must understand this state of imbalance if we want to comprehend the religious developments within the Tokugawa period.

SELECTED READINGS

Boxer, C. R. *The Christian Century in Japan 1549–1650.* The authoritative work on early Roman Catholicism in Japan.

Earhart, H. Byron. *Religion in the Japanese Experience.* See pp. 106–11 for excerpts from Boxer describing the Jesuit experience in Japan, and pp. 121–23 for Hideyoshi's "Letter to the Viceroy of the Indies," in which he rejects Christianity.

Laures, Johannes. *The Catholic Church in Japan.* A popular work by a recognized authority.

Suzuki, Norihisa. "Christianity," in *Japanese Religion,* edited by Ichiro Hori, pp. 71–87. A concise overview of the "foreignness" of Christianity in Japan and its major developments.

Tsunoda, Ryusaku, *et al. Sources of Japanese Tradition.* See Chapter 15 for information concerning Nobunaga, Hideyoshi, Ieyasu, and their policies with regard to Christianity.

13.

The Five Traditions: Development and Mutual Influence

From the earliest period of Japanese religious history the five basic traditions interacted with one another. In the second period of Japanese religious history, we have seen how these traditions developed unique forms within the general context of Japanese religion. Buddhism received new waves of influence from China which were restructured into forms of Japanese Buddhism. Likewise, Confucianism and Taoism continued their process of Japanization. Confucianism gave the semiofficial rationale for the state, along with Buddhism and Shinto. Religious Taoism played an equally important role, but on the level of popular religion. Folk religion interacted with the more organized traditions, and persisted within the beliefs and customs of the people. Shinto was busy borrowing from all these religious streams with the motive of becoming systematized and strengthened so as to compete with the other systems.

This period has been called one of development and elaboration because, with the exception of Christianity, no new religious traditions were introduced. Only new streams of the older traditions were introduced, such as the newer sects of Buddhism. Buddhism became elaborated into a truly Japanese phenomenon.

Shinto also underwent development and elaboration when it discovered that it could appropriate the foreign traditions and, by incorporating them into Shinto, make the native elements into a more complete religious system. Study of Confucian classics led Shinto scholars to a study of the Japanese classics, which in turn led them to support a revival movement for repristinating Shinto.

Religious Taoism, which entered Japanese history mainly in the form of a government bureau controlling the calendar and divination, spread through the countryside in various popular forms. The cosmology of religious Taoism provided a rich resource for cosmological speculation, especially within Shinto. On a more popular level, the Taoistic notions within the adopted Chinese calendar gave rise to many widespread beliefs about what was lucky and unlucky. These Taoistic thoughts and beliefs were carried to the people especially by *hijiri*, a kind of popular successor to the earlier officials in the government bureau of religious

Taoism (the Onmyo-ryo).[1] The *hijiri*, a combination of sage, saint, and fortune teller, were wandering practitioners who went directly to the people to meet all kinds of religious needs. Unattached to either shrines or temples, they drew on Shinto and Buddhist usages as well as those of religious Taoism in their practice of fortune telling, divination, and purifications.

One popular cult which drew heavily on the influence of religious Taoism and the activity of *hijiri* was the Koshin cult. The mythological background of the cult had become mixed with Buddhist elements in China, and was blended with Japanese folk practices by such people as the *hijiri* and local village cults. The village cults were independent associations organized for the purpose of lengthening life through all-night vigils. They met especially on the six Koshin days of the Chinese calendar, revering an image or painting of the Taoist-Buddhist divinity while holding a festive banquet. During the all-night vigils they abstained from sexual relations, because on that night a divinity observed them and reported on their conduct to a heavenly superior. These cults, their beliefs, and practices, became so thoroughly ingrained in village life that the devotees took for granted the Japanese character of the Koshin cult, completely forgetting its foreign origins.

Folk religion continued in the many customs and beliefs associated with seasonal rhythms and the home, but in increasing interaction with the organized religions. The beliefs and festivities of the Chinese calendar were inseparably interwoven with Japanese seasonal and agricultural customs. For example, the New Year festivities came to be celebrated especially through Buddhist and Shinto usages. Popular religious observances connected with the growing season, too, were related to the organized religions. Often a farmer visited a shrine or temple in order to obtain a paper charm which he would place in his rice field as a blessing for his crop.

The home continued to be a major focus for folk religion. This is especially well illustrated by the religious decorations around the home at New Year's. Each household became an unconscious repository of the various religious elements within the Japanese tradition. For example, each family knew that physical and spiritual sickness could be caused by evil forces, which could be warded off through the help of benevolent divinities. The afflicted family might visit a temple or a shrine; or an itinerant *hijiri* or Shugendo practitioner might visit the afflicted family. These popular practitioners resorted to Buddhist rituals and formulas as well as Taoistic purifications in order to effect healing. Some popular religious figures specialized in the art of trance and possession for the purpose of communicating with the dead. Often a blind woman, a kind of female shaman, communicated with the dead. All these practices illustrate the way in which folk religion continued to exist outside of organized religion, while various elements of the organized traditions came to be the common property of the people.

---

[1] For a treatment of the wandering practitioner of "holy-man" called *hijiri*, see Ichiro Hori, "On the Concept of *Hijiri* (Holy-man)."

13. The Five Traditions   *83*

Christianity's appearance on the Japanese scene was an unexpected interruption to this process of development and elaboration. Indeed, in this early period Christianity could hardly be considered a *Japanese* tradition. It is very interesting that those who did not accept Christianity saw it as a threat to all the "Japanese" traditions. In other words, Buddhism, Confucianism, and Shinto took a stand together as Japanese traditions which jointly challenged the threat of the anti-Japanese, or at least non-Japanese, tradition of Christianity.

The process of development and elaboration ran into something of a dead end when it reached the latter part of this second period of religious history. The vital religious motives which impelled the founders of the newer Buddhist sects became crystallized in institutional forms. The problem of institutionalization appears in the history of any religious tradition, calling for a renewal of the wellsprings from which the tradition flows. At this particular juncture in Japanese history, formalism became a widespread problem in all Japanese religion, and yet there appeared no new religious geniuses, such as the founders of the newer Buddhist sects. Because no renewal took place, organized religion tended to stagnate. Eventually, the forms were perpetuated without the spiritual realization of the original religious motives. On the whole, the forms of worship at Shinto shrines and Buddhist temples, and the old formulas for combining Shinto and Buddhism remained the same as centuries before. We will see how this formalism became an even greater problem before it finally provoked movements of renewal, especially within folk religion and Shinto.

SELECTED READINGS

Earhart, H. Byron *Religion in the Japanese Experience.* See Part Eight for selected documents on syncretism in Japan; see also pp. 39–44 for excerpts from Matsunaga, and pp. 76–80 for excerpts from Saunders.

————. *A Religious Study of the Mount Haguro Sect of Shugendo.* Demonstrates the blending of most Japanese religious traditions, both organized and folk, within the life of Shugendo.

Hori, Ichiro. "On the Concept of Hijiri (Holy-man)." Treats the popularization of organized religion through the medium of "holy men."

Matsunaga, Alicia. *The Buddhist Philosophy of Assimilation.* Interprets interaction among religious traditions from the viewpoint of Buddhism.

Saunders, E. Dale. "Koshin; An Example of Taoist Ideas in Japan." Shows how a Taoist cult became thoroughly "Japanized."

Part III

FOSSILIZATION AND RENEWAL IN JAPANESE RELIGION

14.

Buddhism and Neo-Confucianism in the Tokugawa Period, and Restoration Shinto

The Problem of Fossilization and Renewal in Religious History

The long history of every religious tradition includes uneven periods of growth and decline. A new religious tradition may emerge gradually and inconspicuously out of a previous tradition, or it may spring up overnight as the radical discovery of a religious genius. Some new religious traditions soon disappear from history, but those which enjoy permanence must embody the original religious inspiration within lasting forms, that is, become institutionalized. For long periods of time institutionalized forms of religion function effectively to perpetuate the original religious inspiration. Then, either gradually or suddenly, there is the realization that forms are being perpetuated for their own sake and the original religious inspiration has been lost.

As Joachim Wach has described this process, "the very acts which were designed to witness to the highest communion lose their meaning, become, if they are still performed, empty, fossilized." If a religious tradition is to survive the period of fossilization, it must find means for renewal or reform. "Reformation is a universal phenomenon required by the dialectics of religious life."[1] Such

---

[1]Joachim Wach, *Types of Religious Experience Christian and Non-Christian* (Chicago: The University of Chicago Press, 1951), p. 43.

reformation usually features the ideal of a return to some original, pure forms together with some newly conceived forms.

Fossilization and Renewal in Japanese Religious History

Several instances of reformation occurred in the earlier expressions of Japanese Buddhism. Nara Buddhism was reformed by Heian Buddhism in the form of the Tendai and Shingon sects. In the Kamakura period, when the Tendai and Shingon sects tended to become formalistic, or fossilized, the reform movements developed into the Pure Land, Nichiren, and Zen sects. It will be noted that the fossilized forms themselves do not necessarily die out completely. They may regain their former vitality, or they may lie dormant for a long while. The Tendai and Shingon sects never died out, but in the passage of time they were relegated to a place of lesser importance by the newer sects. In one sense the Tendai sect lived on mainly within the reform of the Nichiren and Pure Land sects, all of which claimed the true basis for restoring Tendai to its original inspiration. By the Tokugawa period (1600–1867) the older sects had become extremely formalistic, with no movement of renewal. No new major Buddhist sect appeared from Tokugawa times on, except for the Obaku sect of Zen imported from China in the seventeenth century. In fact, the major Buddhist development after Kamakura times was the proliferation of denominations within the established sects. The denominations tended to capture and crystallize the sect founder and his original inspiration, rather than using these resources creatively to breathe new life into Buddhism.

In terms of religious vitality Shinto was not much better off than Buddhism. The small village shrines tended to remain close to the life of the people, so the masses continued to participate directly in the local religious activities. However, the larger shrines withdrew into the formalism of their own ceremonies. Likewise, the speculative systems constructed by the Shinto scholars did not affect the people.

The formalism within Buddhism and Shinto was a symptom of the need for renewal of a vigorous religious life, yet the decisive answer came from outside these two traditions. Throughout Japanese history popular religion existed outside the organized traditions of Shinto and Buddhism. Elements of religious Taoism, as well as popular Buddhist practices (such as reciting the *nembutsu*), were carried on by the people apart from organized religion. These elements became mixed with agricultural festivals or were absorbed by popular religious leaders, some of whom practiced a kind of shamanism. Especially in Tokugawa times, while Buddhism and Shinto perpetuated the outer forms of religion, the mass of the Japanese people found their religious experience in popular expressions.

In addition to religious factors as such, there were social and economic factors which tended to weaken interest in organized religion and draw many people to more secular pursuits. Toward the end of the Tokugawa period, cities began to grow in size and importance, at the same time that trading and commerce began to outweigh agriculture economically. When many farmers left the countryside for the city, they also removed themselves from the cosmic rhythm of the seasons and fertility. Work for wages in the city meant a different way of life, one that looked increasingly to the life style of the merchant as an ideal. Traditionally merchants were the lowest social class, but by controlling the rice market and the exchange of rice for money, merchants gained such financial power that they even outranked warriors and rivaled the military dictators. Forbidden by law to flaunt their wealth openly, the merchants used their wealth to throw private parties, seek pleasure in geisha houses, and indulge in rather gaudy art works. In general, for both the rich merchant and the average worker, there was at least as much interest in the sensuality of this world as there was in the spirituality of the other world. Interest in the pleasures of this world was reflected in the popularity of ribald novels and wood block prints featuring both daily life and sensual delights.[2] Thus, the Tokugawa period saw a combination of formalism in organized religion and increasing secularism on the part of the people.

Tokugawa Buddhism: State Patronage at the Expense of Weakened Vitality

The Tokugawa period (1600–1867) was able to enjoy peace and order thanks to the unification of the country achieved by the earlier military rulers. The whole period was characterized by stability and conservatism rather than innovation and creativity. The tone of the period was set by the need to maintain the previous unification with a strong central government. A consistent policy of the Tokugawa government was to eliminate religious strife which threatened to divide the country into warring factions. Whereas earlier the military rulers had favored Christianity in order to counteract the power of Buddhism, later in the Tokugawa period Buddhism was patronized in association with a persecution of Christians.

During the Tokugawa period, when Christianity was a proscribed religion, Buddhism was an arm of the government to enforce this proscription. Every family had to belong to a Buddhist temple, and had to be examined periodically by the temple priest. Births were registered and deaths were recorded in the local Buddhist temple to which the family belonged. The Tokugawa government was even responsible for rebuilding many temples destroyed in earlier warfare, including temples at the Tendai headquarters of Hieizan, which had been ruthlessly razed by the earlier ruler Nobunaga. However, the state money which flowed freely into the Buddhist temples cost them their autonomy and religious vitality. The earlier military rulers such as Nobunaga punished the large temples with military force because the temples were the most powerful political rivals. The

---

[2]For a glimpse of this glittering world see Howard S. Hibbett, *The Floating World in Japanese Fiction* (London: Oxford University Press, 1959).

14. Buddhism and Neo-Confucianism 87

Tokugawa government, by unifying the country, simply controlled all the Buddhist sects from the top. Buddhist priests became government servants, and the government strictly forbade any inter-sect quarrels. Buddhism was practically the established religion of Japan, with the separate sects remaining under direct government supervision.

This situation stifled religious devotion. As Anesaki aptly describes the general reaction, "For the people at large religion was rather a matter of family heritage and formal observance than a question of personal faith."[3] To the present day, the organized sects of Japanese Buddhism have not been able to escape completely this unfavorable stigma of disinterested affiliation.

Neo-Confucianism: Political Stability and Social Conformity

The role of Neo-Confucianism in this period must be understood as an intellectual and social force which provided the rationale for the existing social classes and their support of the Tokugawa government. However, the Neo-Confucianism of Tokugawa times must be distinguished from the Confucianism of earlier Japan. Confucianism entered Japan with the flood of Chinese culture which also included Buddhism. In early Japan the Confucian tradition became one of the guiding rationales for the state, as evidenced in the so-called Constitution of Prince Shotoku. Confucian principles helped support reverence for the emperor, and Confucianism gradually came to be considered a Japanese tradition. Nevertheless, until Tokugawa times Confucianism had always played a subordinate role, contributing to the national tradition but not existing as a separate school. In fact, Confucian scholarship was kept alive within the Buddhist temples where Buddhist priests naturally combined an interest in Chinese Buddhist scriptures and the Confucian classics. The scholars of the Zen sects from the thirteenth to seventeenth centuries were most influential in preserving and transmitting the traditions which emerged in Neo-Confucianism.

Neo-Confucianism is a general term for the Confucian revival which took place in China, especially during the Sung dynasty (960–1279). Confucianism in China had already undergone various periods of development. During the Sung dynasty Confucianism borrowed from Taoism and Buddhism to create a comprehensive synthesis for interpreting every aspect of the world and man's life in the world. This synthesis, called Neo-Confucianism, offered a profound understanding of cosmology, humanistic ethics, and political philosophy in one unified system. It enjoyed great success, not only in China, but also in Korea and Japan. Although there were several schools within Neo-Confucianism, the Chinese philosopher Chu Hsi (1130–1200) developed the most famous system of thought. (In Japan, Chu Hsi is called Shushi.)

In early Japan the Confucian classics were adopted as the basis of education,

---

[3]Masharu Anesaki, *History of Japanese Religion,* p. 260.

and were studied from Nara times up to the Tokugawa period. However, these studies became stagnant and scholastic since they continued to depend upon Chinese commentaries composed many centuries previously. Gradually the tradition of Neo-Confucianism maintained within the Japanese Zen temples began to attract attention outside Buddhist circles, influencing even the hereditary Confucian scholars. The pre-eminence of Neo-Confucian philosophy became official in 1647 when the emperor commanded the hereditary Confucian scholars to use the commentaries of the Sung dynasty and disregard the earlier commentaries. This official pronouncement recognized as the prevailing rationale of the state the philosophy of Chu Hsi, or Shushi. However, the real importance of this philosophy was not its connection with the imperial line, but its foundational character for the Tokugawa feudal regime.

The Tokugawa government was more interested in the organizational powers of Neo-Confucianism than its cosmological theories. Tokugawa Ieyasu (1542–1616) apparently saw in Neo-Confucianism a suitable philosophy for stabilizing and ordering the state. In this context what the Neo-Confucian tradition amounted to was a heavenly sanction for the existing political and social order. The rulers or superiors were advised to be just and benevolent, whereas the subordinates were cautioned to be obedient and respectful. The harmony of the universe depended upon a reciprocal relationship of justice on the part of the superior and obedience on the part of the subordinate. One venerable Confucian scheme for working out this harmony in greater detail was the bond of five human relationships. These five sets of relationships are ruler and subject, parents and children, husband and wife, elder and younger, and, finally, friend and friend. The last relationship, friendship, is characterized by mutuality; the other four relationships are characterized by the general rule of the obedience of subordinates to superiors. This philosophy was very important for informing the feudalistic ethics of Tokuwaga times. While Neo-Confucianism did not create the feudal situation, it provided the supporting rationale.

There has been criticism of the political use of the Confucian (or Neo-Confucian) tradition simply to justify the status quo; there is no doubt that Neo-Confucianism in Japan played its role in helping to maintain the peace during this time. Neo-Confucianism contributed especially to social mores and education. A famous example is the Neo-Confucian contribution to the philosophy of life called Bushido, the "way of the warrior," a scheme of training and code of ethics that emphasized, above all, self-control and duty to one's master. It also included the aspect of self-cultivation. While at first it was limited mainly to the class of warriors, this combined sense of frugality and unswerving loyalty later had wide influence among the people. However, the personal qualities of loyalty and filial piety had been stressed in earlier Japanese history, and Neo-Confucianism only reinforced them. The Japanese *samurai* (warrior), too, drew upon several traditions simultaneously. "The typical Tokugawa samurai saw some value in each of the three world views that competed for his allegiance.

Buddhism and Shinto provided for his religious needs; Confucianism gave him a rational cosmology and a social ethic; Confuciansm and Shinto both contributed to his conceptions of the political order."[4]

Under Tokugawa patronage Neo-Confucianism became a combination of state cult and state educational system. By this time there were independent scholars of Neo-Confucianism outside the Buddhist temples. These scholars were given land on which to found Neo-Confucian schools: the schools not only studied the Chinese classics by means of the Neo-Confucian commentaries, but provided bureaucrats for the Tokugawa government. The cultic aspect is seen in the fact that these same scholars were ordered to perform the old Confucian ceremonies such as the annual sacrifices, and Confucian temples were built for these sacrifices. The Chu Hsi school of Neo-Confucianism enjoyed such privileged protection by the government that other schools of Neo-Confucianism were outlawed. In general, Neo-Confucianism exerted a widespread influence, tending to move away from Buddhism and combine forces with the earlier attempts to purify Shinto. Likewise popular teachers arose who established schools in which great numbers of the middle class were instructed in a heavily Neo-Confucian inspired philosophy of life.

Restoration Shinto: The Movement for a Purified Shinto

Shinto had been overshadowed by the more highly systematized foreign traditions among the court and nobility ever since the sixth century, but it had remained vital to the religious life of the local communities. Even during the most flourishing periods of Buddhism, there were Shinto scholars who remained true to their Shinto heritage. In medieval times Kitabatake Chikafusa wrote a theological defense of the divine ancestry of the emperor and the centrality of Japan in Shinto conceptions. Indeed, the medieval schools of Shinto, though borrowing heavily from foreign traditions, had as their ultimate goal the improvement of Shinto's inferior role in Japanese religion. There had always been some support for Shinto among the "royalists," the persons around the imperial court who favored the return of the emperor to actual power. It is only natural that those of the court were opposed to rule by a military leader and his warriors, and there were religious commitments on both sides of this opposition. The several lines of Shinto support were united and reinforced in Tokugawa times by a powerful movement called Restoration Shinto.

Restoration Shinto was not a simple resuscitation of Shinto, since it had never died out; nor was it a sudden awakening. It was the culmination of the work of previous centuries and previous scholars, stimulated by several peculiar condi-

---

[4]John Whitney Hall, "The Confucian Teacher in Tokugawa Japan," p. 291. An excerpt from this article is included in H. Byron Earhart, *Religion in the Japanese Experience,* pp. 66–69.

tions of Tokugawa times. For one thing, the isolation of Japan from foreign influence for about two centuries had a positive as well as a negative result. While foreign influence was excluded, the feeling of national pride and national strength was reinforced. Another stimulation for Restoration Shinto came from Neo-Confucianism. It must be remembered that Neo-Confucianism had to divorce itself from the Buddhist temples in order to become an independent movement, so it was more favorably diposed to Shinto than to Buddhism. In addition, Neo-Confucianism had become thoroughly Japanized, such that its main goal was to support the Japanese tradition and the political system. Neo-Confucianism encouraged and supported the policy of isolating Japan from the world. Thus, Neo-Confucianism and Shinto shared a common goal of glorifying the Japanese nation. Interest in the Chinese classics stimulated interest in the Japanese classics. Eventually Shinto developed such a high degree of self-consciousness that it rejected all foreign influence, including its former ally of Neo-Confucianism.

The interest in Japanese classics was placed on firmer ground when Kada Azumamaro (1669–1736) started a school of National Learning for the purpose of studying Japan's own literature. This led the way for two of the leading scholars of Japanese language and literature, Kamo Mabuchi (1697–1769) and Motoori Norinaga (1730–1801). All ancient Japanese writings, including not only the *Kojiki* and *Nihongi,* but also valuable poetry and novels, had been neglected for so long that few persons could read or understand them. In fact, the ancient literature had become buried under a mantle of Chinese and Buddhist interpretation. Mabuchi and Motoori made a great achievement in discarding the current Buddhist and Chinese clichés in order to approach the literature for its own worth. They succeeded in showing that this early poetry and literature did not conform to abstract Buddhist or Confucian ideals, but reflected the "true" Japanese spirit before it had become "spoiled" by foreign influences. Implicit in this criticism was the idea that everything Japanese had been natural, spontaneous, and pure; foreign influence was artificial in the sense of destroying naturalness and purity. The tone of the criticism was often irrational, even mystical, in advocating a return to the original state of purity from which the Japanese had fallen. In terms of religion, this meant a restoration of Shinto as the true Japanese religion, purified of its foreign borrowings, and in terms of politics, a restoration of imperial rule. In late Tokugawa times these patterns of thought became linked with a general dissatisfaction for the Tokugawa government and formed the basis for an ultranationalistic movement. Already in Tokugawa times the need for religious renewal had resulted in the appearance of several New Religions, which will be discussed in later chapters.

SELECTED READINGS

Bellah, Robert N. *Tokugawa Religion.* A sociological analysis of a highly eclectic Tokugawa movement; this author argues for the existence of a kind of "Protestant ethic" in Japan.

14. Buddhism and Neo-Confucianism   *91*

Earhart, H. Byron. *Religion in the Japanese Experience.* See Part Fifteen for the dilemma of Shinto and Buddhism as organized religions in modern Japan (including excerpts from Tsukamoto's article).

Eliot, Sir Charles. *Japanese Buddhism.* See pp. 305–17 for a description of increasing formalism in Japanese Buddhism.

Holtom, Daniel C. See pp. 44–52 for a brief treatment of Restoration Shinto (treated as "Renaissance Shinto").

Kishimoto, Hideo, and Wakimoto, Tsuneya. "Introduction: Religion During Tokugawa." A critical overview of religion in the Tokugawa period.

Matsumoto, Shigeru. *Motoori Norinaga: 1730–1801.* A detailed study of the foremost scholar and proponent of Restoration Shinto.

Smith, Warren W., Jr. *Confucianism in Modern Japan.* See pp. 6–40 for a historical summary of Neo-Confucianism in the Tokugawa period.

Tsukamoto, Zenryu. "Japanese and Chinese Buddhism." A leading Buddhist scholar's critical analysis of the stagnation of "formalized Buddhism" in Tokugawa times.

Tsunoda, Ryusaku, *et al. Sources of Japanese Tradition.* See Chapters 16, 17, and 18 for translated documents concerning Neo-Confucianism in Japan.

15.

The Meiji Restoration and Nationalistic Shinto

The Political and Religious Significance of the Meiji Restoration

The Meiji Restoration of 1868 is of tremendous importance in understanding modern Japan and modern Japanese religion. Perhaps the greatest significance of the Meiji Restoration is the ending of the Tokugawa feudalism and the founding of the modern Japanese state. For more than two hundred years the Tokugawa rulers had maintained peace in the country on a feudal basis, but increasingly it was unable to rule the country effectively. Economically, there were severe problems of indebtedness, which led to widespread suffering and resulted in peasant uprisings. In addition, toward the end of the Tokugawa period there was the political threat of foreign insistence upon open trade with Japan. As the Tokugawa government became more inefficient in meeting these pressing problems, the insistence for restoration of the emperor became more popular. There had always been factions supporting the emperor against the Tokugawa ruler, and now these factions were reinforced by several new developments. The attempt to link the Tokugawa government and the imperial family was unsuccessful. There was growing dissatisfaction with Neo-Confucianism as a means of regulating the country, and growing interest in the study of Western science.

As the result of these complex factors, the Tokugawa government was defeated and the emperor was "restored," at least in name, to his rightful position as head of state. The Meiji Restoration drew its name from this reinstallment of the emperor, but in actuality it was no simple repristination. On the contrary, the Meiji period (1868–1912) marks the dividing line between feudal Japan and modern Japan. The whole system of government was reorganized along the lines of a nation-state. The office of the military ruler was abolished and the emperor formally ruled a centralized government with a constitution and elected legislators. The feudal clans were replaced with prefectures which administered local government as a branch of the central authority. The new capital was established at Tokyo. To finance the government a tax system was adopted. It was obvious that if the central government was to be sovereign, feudal armies would have to be replaced with an imperial or national army. These radical transformations in politics and economics took time, requiring adjustment of sincere ideals to realistic possibility.

In conjunction with the political and economic changes of the Meiji Restoration, there were significant changes in the realm of religion. The religious transition from Tokugawa times into the Meiji era, if oversimplified, can be described as the replacement of state patronage of Buddhism with state patronage of Shinto (or nationalistic Shinto). However, as in the realm of politics and economics, the religious transition took time and involved experimentation with several varying arrangements. In general there was a negative purpose in demoting Buddhism and a positive purpose in elevating Shinto.

The motive for demoting Buddhism is easily understood, since Buddhism had been, in effect, a branch of the Tokugawa feudal government. Furthermore, the financial corruption and spiritual decadence of Buddhism were sufficiently recognized to make it an easy target for the reforming zeal of the Meiji architects. The motive for elevating Shinto is obvious, too, even though it was a difficult policy to implement. The general notion was that just as the emperor had been restored to his rightful status as (titular) head of the state, so should Shinto be restored to its rightful position as the old imperial religion—and new state religion.

In the transitional period there was an exaggerated zeal against the old regime and Buddhism, accompanied by an exaggerated enthusiasm with the program of the newly restored Shinto. Up until the Meiji period a majority of Shinto shrines had been under heavy Buddhist influence. This was only natural, since Shinto shrines and Buddhist temples were built side-by-side, and the priests of the two traditions cooperated in the worship of both edifices. However, during the Tokugawa period, high-ranking Buddhist priests often came to control Shinto shrines. In reaction to this situation, many Meiji reformers were outspoken in their aim of "purifying" Shinto from the foreign influence of Buddhism. Japan has always presented a baffling mixture of the old and the new; the Meiji Restoration attempted its own blend of old and new. It sought to return to the pure, original Japanese government and religion, while at the same time boldly opening Japan to all kinds of new, foreign ideas and usages.

The Attempt to Repristinate Shinto as the Only Japanese Religion

Restoration meant purifying Shinto shrines and the Shinto priesthood from Buddhist influence. Buddhist statues were removed from shrines and Buddhist priests ejected. However, the proximity between the two priesthoods is further illustrated by this very move: Many Buddhist priests simply renounced their Buddhist ordination and overnight became Shinto priests! For a while Buddhism actually suffered from persecution. There was a widespread cry to eliminate Buddhism and Buddhist monks. Many priceless Buddhist treasures were wantonly destroyed, while others were bought for a pittance to become the nucleus of Western museum collections. Nevertheless, even when Buddhist faith was at its lowest ebb, Buddhism could not be completely eliminated from Japan. The stubborn persistence of Buddhism was one factor which dampened the early enthusiasm for the Shinto restoration.

In general, one can say that as Buddhism was disestablished, Shinto was established. The ideal was to return to the earlier period when Shinto had played a prominent role in government. Accordingly, in 1868 Shinto was proclaimed the sole basis of the government. Not only was the emperor the head of the state (and the imperial rituals were state rituals), but there was also a Department of Shinto within the government which was superior to other departments. In addition to purifying Shinto from Buddhist influence, the department began to regulate Shinto on a centralized, nationwide basis. For example, the hereditary succession of Shinto priests was abolished so that all Shinto priests could be appointed by the Department of Shinto as government officials. Shinto priests were used to propagate purified Shinto, especially in the districts where Buddhist influence was strongest.

An imperial rescript proclaimed in 1870 explained the rationale for such policies. According to the rescript, the Japanese nation had been founded by the gods (*kami*) and preserved by an unbroken line of emperors who maintained "the unity of religion and state." This unity of religion and state was considered indispensable for the restoration activities of the Meiji era. By 1871 there was an official policy of using Shinto parishes for registration purposes, instead of the Buddhist parishes of Tokugawa times. After the expulsion of Christianity, the government required every family to belong to a Buddhist temple of their choice, to insure the prohibition of Christianity. In the early Meiji period, the new government required every person to register at a local Shinto shrine, at birth and upon change of residence. Utilization of the Shinto parish system was more positive in nature, since its purpose was to unify the state, rather than to attack Buddhism or Christianity.

It is difficult to imagine the turmoil and disorder which accompanied the transition from feudal to modern times. The Meiji government, or at least one major faction, sought to order the chaotic situation by returning to the ideals of Shinto. However, neither government order nor intellectual persuasion was able to reduce the complex religious history of Japan into a completely Shinto affair. Some people feared (and some hoped) that Buddhism was doomed for extinction, together with the Tokugawa feudal regime. But the criticism and persecution of Buddhism had a purging effect. Although caught at its lowest ebb of spiritual resources, Japanese Buddhism rallied to fight for its own role in helping to create the new modern state. In fact, Buddhism became more active than Shinto in developing an apologetic against the Christian missionaries of the Meiji era.

Two basic factors persuaded the new government to back down from its exaggerated enthusiasm for Shinto as the sole foundation of the state. First, there was the renewed strength of Japanese Buddhism with Japan, and second, there was the clamor for religious freedom in Japan by foreign spokesmen. The renewed strength of Buddhism made it impossible for the Department of Shinto to handle both Shinto and Buddhist affairs. Therefore, the Department of Shinto was abolished, and between 1872 and 1875 there was a brief attempt to administer both Shinto and Buddhism within a newly created Department of Religion. Nevertheless, it was impractical to try to reunify Shinto and Buddhism in the joint

15. Meiji Restoration and Nationalistic Shinto

administration of the Department of Religion. In 1877 the Department of Religion was abolished and a temporary Bureau of Shrines and Temples lasted until the official designation of "shrine Shinto" in 1882. (Buddhism's vitality between 1868 and 1882 forced the government to recognize Buddhism as well as Shinto.)

Christianity was another factor which made it impossible to recognize Shinto as the only religion in Japan. With the official opening of Japan to foreign intercourse in 1868, Christian missionaries (both Catholic and Protestant) entered Japan. Technically, the Tokugawa proscription of Christianity had not yet been lifted. At this time Japan, emerging from a seclusion of about two centuries, was very sensitive to foreign criticism. Government missions went abroad to observe the functioning of Western countries so that the Meiji government could be established on sound lines. The Japanese officials desired to copy Western practices which they thought were beneficial to Japan, and actively sought to establish relations with Western nations. On the other hand, Western diplomats pleaded for the reintroduction of Christianity into Japan. With this background of Western insistence, and possibly stimulated by the more liberal minds of the Meiji era, in 1873 the ban against Christianity was lifted. Christianity was a recognized religion and Christian missionaries could legally enter Japan. At the same time the regulation for compulsory registration at Shinto shrines was dropped. From about 1875 the government attitude toward religion shifted to a new direction.

The Establishment of Nonreligious Shrine Shinto

In effect, officials of the new government decided that if they could not make Shinto the sole religion of the state, then they would make the state into a semi-Shinto institution. This meant that Shinto was just as deeply involved in state matters, but the state declared Shinto to be nonreligious in character. To be more precise, a law of 1882 divided Shinto into shrine Shinto (sometimes called nationalistic, or state Shinto by Western writers) and sect Shinto. Under the category of shrine Shinto the law included most of the Shinto shrines throughout the country, excluding only the shrines which had developed special sect forms. (This government action did not create any new shrines, but rather, changed the status of most local shrines.) From 1882 only shrine Shinto could call their buildings shrines (*jinja*) since they alone were state institutions. A special Bureau of Shrines was set up in the Department of Home Affairs to deal with the administration of the shrines as state institutions. All other religious movements and the sect developments of Shinto were treated separately as religions.

Under the category of sect Shinto were included thirteen groups which had developed as sect branches of Shinto, or had accepted Shinto forms in order to gain government recognition as independent sects. The thirteen branches of sect Shinto were considered by the government as religions. The buildings of sect Shinto could not be called shrines, but were called *kyokai*, a term usually translated as "church." This placed sect Shinto in the realm of religions, just like the religious sects of Buddhism and Christianity. In fact all these religions (shrine Shinto being excluded from the definition of religion) were supervised by a Bureau of Religions within the Department of Education.

This policy, on the surface a separation of religion and state, was of great convenience to the Meiji government. It paid lip service to religious freedom, since technically no religion was required and no religion was prohibited; at the same time it provided a free hand for using the supposedly nonreligious shrine Shinto to unify the country through patriotic support of the state. The Constitution of 1899 guaranteed religious freedom, which was attainable as long as shrine Shinto was considered nonreligious. On the other hand, the Imperial Rescript on Education of 1890 assured that Shinto and Confucian principles would be respected in the moral education of the people in order to unify the nation.[1] The Rescript enjoined loyalty to the state as a corollary of reverence for the imperial ancestors who founded it. The Rescript did not advocate a new tradition, but its teaching was used as a powerful tool in every Japanese school to instill reverence for the emperor and unquestioning loyalty to the state. It is to be remembered that "religious" teaching as defined by the state, meaning especially Buddhist and Christian teaching, was excluded from schools. In general, shrine Shinto was supported politically and economically by the government. Theoretically the religions should have been free to manage their own affairs, but in practice they were restricted or even suppressed.

Shrine Shinto as an Expression of Nationalistic Militarism

This kind of shrine Shinto has been called nationalistic Shinto by Westerners because it was used as a major support to the Japanese nationalism which preceded World War II. Most Japanese people who grew up after 1890 received a public education of nationalistic ethics. Those who questioned absolute loyalty to the state were definitely in the minority: some liberal intellectuals, a few of the so-called New Religions, and a few Christians. The 1890 Rescript on Education had been prompted by a reaction to excessive Westernization; about 1930 another surge of antiforeign feeling swept the country. Especially after about 1930, when Japan's relations with foreign countries deteriorated, it became a serious matter to question the state's authority. In 1938 all schools were required to use an ultranationalistic textbook which emphasized the uniqueness and supremacy of Japan as a political and religious unity; in Japanese this "national entity" is called *kokutai.*[2]

The question of nationalism is a delicate one, because the bad memory of World War II is still with us. Many Western treatments of Shinto, written prior

---

[1]For a translation of "The Imperial Rescript on Education," see H. Byron Earhart, *Religion in the Japanese Experience,* pp. 203–4.

[2]See John Owen Gauntlett for a translation of this text, *Kokutai no Hongi. Cardinal Principles of the National Entity of Japan.*

to and during World War II, tended to depict Shinto as the sole source of Japanese nationalism and the cause of the war. Even today in the United States there remains a popular conception that the cause of the war was Shinto: According to the popular Western conception, because Shinto commanded worship of an emperor-god, the Japanese soldiers were bound to follow the emperor's command to extend the Japanese empire into foreign lands. However, this exaggeration is more representative of American wartime fears than of the actual situation in Japan.

In the several decades since the end of World War II there has been a reassessment of Shinto and its relationship to nationalism and militarism. Earlier Western notions of Shinto probably placed too much emphasis on the nationalistic aspects of Shinto and linked Shinto too closely to its manipulation by the government; this misconception tended to view the essence of Shinto itself as the particular unity of state and Shinto during the past century. But to call this "state Shinto," and then to think of it as indicating the nature of Shinto through its long history, is obviously a mistake. It is more difficult, but more true to the facts, to try to distinguish between the perennial tie of Shinto to the Japanese identity, and the modern manipulation of this tie for militaristic purposes. Another inadequacy of "state Shinto" as a blanket term is that it fails to differentiate between the intentions of the government administrators, the shrine priests, and the people at large. It is quite likely that these three groups often participated within the same governmentally controlled shrines, but each with different intentions. The government administrators might have been concerned mainly with ideological control of the populace; the shrine priests might have had in mind ritual and theological concerns; and the people may have looked to simple blessing of their homes and welfare.

One of the problems in reassessing modern Shinto is the lack of precise terms differentiating traditional Shinto from its nationalistic involvement. Among the attempts at reappraising Shinto, one scholar has proposed separating the discussion of the "Kokutai cult" from the topic of Shinto as such. Kokutai cult is defined as "Japan's emperor-state-centered cult of ultranationalism and militarism" which "included elements of Shinto mythology and ideology and . . . utilized Shinto institutions and practices," but "was not a form of Shinto." Defined in this manner, the Kokutai cult consisted of six elements compulsory for all Japanese: 1) "acceptance of the doctrine that the Emperor was 'sacred and inviolable,' " 2) veneration or worship of spirits of the imperial ancestors and imperial rescripts; 3) unquestioned acceptance of ancient myths and their chauvinistic interpretation in modern works such as the nationalistic textbook *Kokutai no Hongi;* 4) the observance of national holidays, centering in the glorification of the imperial line; 5) worship of *kami* at shrines and in the home (before the *kamidana*); 6) financial support of local shrines and festivals.[3] This interpretation

---

[3]William P. Woodard, *The Allied Occupation of Japan 1945–1952 and Japanese Religions,* p. 11.

III. FOSSILIZATION AND RENEWAL

highlights the complexities of the relationship of Shinto to nationalism; it also demonstrates the need for an understanding of nationalism in Japan.

The background factors of nationalism in Japan, like the causes of war, are many and complex: They include the whole context of economic, political, and social conditions in prewar Japan. One scholar who has studied nationalism in Japan claims that nationalism can be fostered by one or more of a number of elements. These elements are geographical separateness, common racial descent (actual or supposed), a common language, and common religious beliefs. His conclusion is that, "Although few nations are influenced by all the recognized elements of nationalism, in Japan each of the elements not only is present but exists in an unusually strong form."[4] Shinto was but one of the contributing factors to Japan's ultranationalism. In fact, the pioneer Western scholar of Shinto nationalism, D. C. Holtom, has shown that Japanese Buddhism competed with Shinto in claiming to support and protect the nation. "If . . . Buddhism has never declared a holy war, it has nonetheless proclaimed all Japanese wars holy."[5] Even Japanese Christians were quick to announce their support of the state program. The ironies of history present a much stranger case. The Chinese tradition of Confucianism had become so Japanized through the centuries that the Japanese could appeal to Confucianism as their own rationale for their "benevolent rule" of Manchuria and Korea. Especially after 1933 Confucianism in Japan became an important rationale for supporting ultranationalism and militarism.[6]

During the first four decades of the twentieth century, Japan's energies were heavily concentrated on the strengthening of nationalism and militarism, and religion, especially Shinto, was used to further these aims. However, proper historical perspective is crucial if we are to understand Shinto: We must see shrine Shinto as a modern development within a tradition with a much longer history. We should avoid the temptation to see the whole history of Shinto in terms of its modern nationalistic phase. For, although shrine Shinto captured the limelight in the modern period, in the countryside Shinto shrines preserved much of the traditional religious life. The major activities at local shrines repeated the old-age pattern: such events as annual festivals for spring and fall associated with agriculture, the elaborate New Year's celebrations, and special village-wide festivities invoking the blessing of the *kami*. While nationalism pervaded even these local Shinto shrines, it represented an overlay directed by the central government, but did not eliminate the age-old religious life of the shrines.

In summary, Shinto (in its modern form of shrine Shinto) tended to dominate other religious traditions in the period from 1868 to 1945, a period in which nationalism, and then ultranationalism combined with militarism, was the key-

---

[4]Delmer M. Brown, *Nationalism in Japan,* pp. 2–7, 12.

[5]Daniel C. Holtom, *Modern Japan and Shinto Nationalism,* p. 148.

[6]See Warren W. Smith, Jr., *Confucianism in Modern Japan;* an excerpt from Smith (which illustrates the role of Confucianism in Japanese nationalism) is included in H. Byron Earhart, *Religion in the Japanese Experience,* pp. 69–74.

15. Meiji Restoration and Nationalistic Shinto   *99*

note of Japanese life. Because of shrine Shinto's dominance over Shinto as a whole, and shrine Shinto's close association with the war effort, after the surrender of 1945 many Japanese people themselves lost trust in Shinto. Nevertheless, nationalistic religion was not the problem of Shinto alone. In early Japanese history as well as before World War II, Buddhism and Confucianism were equally aligned with the national welfare. In the next two chapters we will see how the increasing formalization of religion in Japan heightened the need for a renewal of religious life.

SELECTED READINGS

Brown, Delmer M. *Nationalism in Japan.* A historical study of the complex development of nationalism in Japan.

Earhart, H. Byron. *Religion in the Japanese Experience.* See Part Fourteen for selected documents on the close relation between religion and state, including The Imperial Rescript on Education and excerpts from *Kokutai no Hongi;* see also pp. 218–22 for excerpts from the article by Hori and Toda, and pp. 69–74 for excerpts from Smith.

Fridell, Wilbur M. *Japanese Shrine Mergers 1906–12. State Shinto Moves to the Grassroots.* A detailed analysis of state Shinto in terms of shrine mergers.

Gauntlett, John Owen, trans. *Kokutai no Hongi: Cardinal Principles of the National Entity of Japan.* A translation of the nationalistic textbook used in public schools after 1938.

Holtom, Daniel C. *Modern Japan and Shinto Nationalism.* Contains historical information on nationalistic Shinto, including the nationalistic activities of Christianity and Buddhism in Japan.

Hori, Ichiro, and Toda, Yoshio. "Shinto." A brief critical treatment of Shinto in the Meiji period.

Tsunoda, Ryusaku, *et al. Sources of Japanese Tradition.* See Chapters 24–27 for the variety of liberalism and nationalism from pre-Meiji times to 1945.

Smith, Warren W., Jr. *Confucianism in Japan.* See pp. 41–102 for the role of Confucianism during the Meiji period.

Woodard, William P. *The Allied Occupation of Japan 1945–1952 and Japanese Religions.* See especially pp. 7–13 for "The Occupation and the Kokutai Cult."

16.
Religious Currents from 1868 to 1945: Buddhism, Christianity, and the New Religions

Ultranationalism in Prewar Japan

In the period from 1868 (marking the Meiji Restoration and the reopening of Japan to the West) to 1945 (marking the end of World War II), nationalism pervaded every aspect of Japanese life. From about 1890 the government exerted increasing control over organized religion; prior to World War II the government laid down strict rules for the consolidation of denominations (both Buddhist and Christian) in order to control them more effectively. Shinto, especially shrine Shinto, was a main channel for this nationalism, but other religious traditions were equally affected. Indeed, one scholar feels that after 1933 Confucianism played an even greater role in supporting the national polity (*kokutai*). Confucianism defined the central theme of the book *Kokutai no Hongi*, a nationalistic textbook which was made required reading in all schools after 1938.[1] In the previous chapter Buddhism and even Christianity were also cited as being heavily influenced by the nationalistic movement. However, it would be a mistake to see the religious history of this period only in terms of nationalism. A brief description of Buddhism, Christianity, and the New Religions reveals important religious undercurrents in addition to the major current of nationalism. These undercurrents are important, not only for understanding the prewar period, but especially for understanding the critical spiritual mood of postwar Japan.

Buddhism: The Struggle for Renewal, Especially Within Buddhist Scholarship

With the Meiji Restoration of 1868 Buddhism was faced with an unexpected crisis. Several centuries of patronage by the Tokugawa government (1600–1867) resulted in the Buddhist priests and temples taking for granted their superior positions of wealth and leisure. They seemed so firmly entrenched that financial corruption and spiritual lassitude went unchecked. Then in a flash the Tokugawa government fell and an important source of their income vanished. It was bad enough that the Meiji Restoration did not stop short with a mere reform of

---

[1]See Warren W. Smith, Jr., *Confucianism in Modern Japan*, pp. 156ff. See also John Owen Gauntlett, trans., *Kokutai no Hongi: Cardinal Principles of the National Entity of Japan*.

Buddhism, but instead chose to disestablish Buddhism and to establish Shinto in its place. Even worse, perhaps, was the severe criticism and persecution of Buddhism stimulated by the zeal to restore Shinto. It is true that some of the destruction of Buddhist temples during the transitional period can be attributed to the misplaced enthusiasm which accompanies any radical social change. On the other hand, much of the criticism against Buddhism—financial and moral corruption—was justified.

At first the Buddhist priests could comprehend neither the socio-political transformation nor the criticism against Buddhism. As a whole, Buddhism tried to maintain in the Meiji period the same role and position it had known during the Tokugawa period: religiously, preoccupation with ancestral rites, and politically, subservience to the state. Buddhist priests were so preoccupied with funerals and masses that they were jokingly referred to as the "undertakers of Japan"; they strove to be at least second to Shinto as the supporters of the state. However, implicit in the Meiji criticism of Buddhism was the call for a spiritual as well as a moral renewal of Buddhism. To a certain extent Japanese Buddhism today is still wrestling with this problem of spiritual renewal.

Japanese Buddhism's popular vitality in the early Meiji period was illustrated by the fact that the government was forced to recognize Buddhism as a religion of the people. Nor did Buddhism lack devout and far-sighted priests. Some priests, rather than lamenting the persecution of Buddhism, recognized Buddhism's disestablishment as a blessing in disguise. They had the courage to acknowledge the criticisms leveled against Buddhism, and advocated a spiritual refounding of Japanese Buddhism.

In actuality, Japanese Buddhism was threatened from several sides simultaneously. Shinto strove to abolish or suppress Buddhism as a decadent and foreign religion. Christianity attacked Buddhism on doctrinal grounds. In addition, Buddhism was thrown into the same position as Confucianism, threatened with extinction by the onslaught of Western science and philosophy. While Buddhism's competition with Shinto can be seen in the familiar pattern of nationalistic religion, Buddhism's encounter with Western learning and Christianity must be seen as a remarkable innovation in Japanese religious history.

Buddhist priests accepted the challenge of Western learning by sending priest-scholars to Europe. As early as 1876 Nanjo Bunyu went to England to study Sanskrit texts with Max Müller. This marked an important meeting of East and West, since Müller was the founder of the "science of religion" in Europe, and Nanjo was the first Japanese Buddhist to adopt Western methods of historical and philological scholarship. From this time forward the Buddhist priest-scholars who studied in the best European universities (and published in French, German, or English) strengthened their native erudition with the critical methods of European scholarship (especially those of history and philology). On the Japanese side this scholarly cooperation had two positive results. The reforming desire of devout Buddhists was rewarded with a direct knowledge of early Indian Buddhism. Formerly their knowledge of Buddhism had been filtered through Chinese

Buddhism. A second positive result was a growing confidence in Western methods of critical scholarship and Western philosophy. The Buddhist scholars were competent in relating comparable philosophical movements in the European and Buddhist traditions. Also they were fully capable of using one philosophy to criticize another. During this upsurge of scholarly activity, monumental publishing ventures were undertaken, among which are: the reprinting of the Buddhist canon (in Chinese), compilation of documents from Japanese Buddhism, and publication of erudite encyclopedias and reference works on all aspects of Buddhism.

On the whole, Buddhist priests have been much more in touch with Western culture than Shinto priests. With the establishment of Western-style universities in the Meiji era, Buddhist priests came to be trained in departments of Indian and Buddhist philosophy where the classical languages of Buddhism (Pali and Sanskrit), and also modern European languages, were emphasized. Buddhist appropriation of Western learning and cooperation with Western scholars represented one of the most remarkable possibilities for the renewal of Buddhism in the prewar period.

This possibility for renewal, however, only further complicated an already complex Japanese Buddhism: it was split between traditional piety and modern intellectualism. Popular Buddhism continued in the same patterns as in Tokugawa times, while some Buddhist priests and intellectuals tended to think in terms of appropriated Western concepts. It is worth noting that about this time the systematic or "scientific" study of religion was founded in Japan. This established the academic study of religion apart from such traditional fields as Shinto studies, Buddhist studies, and Chinese studies. Anesaki Masaharu was the first occupant of the chair of the science of religion at Tokyo University in 1905. Some Shinto scholars, notably Kato Genchi, furthered the Japanese study of the science of religion by pioneering Shinto studies in the light of comparative research. These new currents of thought did not affect the people at large, but they did confuse many intellectuals, especially the scholars and students who had accepted Christianity.

Christianity: Strength and Weakness Since 1868

The story of Christianity in Japan from 1868 to 1945 shows some similarities with the Christian century of Roman Catholic missions from about 1550 to 1650. In both periods there were earlier phases of Christian success linked with Japanese acceptance of Western culture, followed by phases of Christianity's decline due to Japanese reaction against the West. Apart from these general similarities, there were some remarkable dissimilarities in the two periods. For example, in the later period, Protestant as well as Roman Catholic missionaries came to Japan.

Christian missionaries arrived in Japan in the late 1850s, soon after the signing of treaties with Western powers. However, they were unable to achieve results until 1873 when the Tokugawa ban on Christianity was lifted. Between

1868 and 1872 there had been several arrests of Christians, especially Catholics.

After 1873 Christianity tended to gain followers. However, the fortune of Christianity in Japan seems to have been dominated by three major factors, which made it difficult to gain individual converts to Christianity, but which at the same time made Christianity an important contribution to the formation of the new Japanese government. The first factor is that the official attitude of Christianity in meeting other traditions has usually been to favor conversion to Christianity rather than syncretism with the other tradition. The blending of Christianity with other traditions has occasionally taken place, but usually on an unofficial basis and over a long period of time. This uncompromising claim for an ethical response to Christian monotheism meant that the Japanese individual had to make a radical leap from his own tradition to accept Christianity. (By contrast, both Buddhism and Confucianism were decidedly syncretistic in their contact with Japanese culture and religion.) The second factor is that the Japanese people were not only self-conscious but proud of their long, unique heritage. To be Japanese usually meant to participate in this heritage, including semireligious activities such as respect for (or veneration of) the emperor, and also participation in Shinto and Japanese Buddhism. From 1868 to 1945 there was an active discussion as to whether one could be both a devout Christian and a loyal Japanese. The third factor was that Japanese officials looked to the West for models of government and science. This meant an initial acceptance of Christianity as the spiritual culture of the West, until the time when the Japanese saw that they could become Westernized (and industrialized) without becoming Christianized.

The social turmoil after 1868 turned many defeated warriors (*samurai*) of the feudal lords to Christianity. Having lost their effort to maintain the Tokugawa government and state Buddhism, they turned to Christianity as a means of ordering Meiji society and government. Some scholars have thought that the religious fervor and courageous loyalty of these early Christians was as much a carry-over from their Confucian warrior training as it was a product of their Christian conversion. At any rate, the Christian faith spread to the middle classes of the cities, so that, already in the 1870s, evangelism was carried out by Japanese Christians. These sincere Japanese Christians were eager to avoid denominationalism, favored financial self-support of Japanese churches, and tried to eliminate Western customs which hindered development of a true Japanese Christianity. They quickly attained almost complete financial independence, but the problems of denominationalism and a truly Japanese Christianity have persisted to the present. For example, the famous Japanese Christian Uchimura (1861–1930) is noted for his statement about his love for the "two J's": "I love two J's and no third; one is Jesus, and the other is Japan."[2] However, his example of blending

---

[2]Ryusaku Tsunoda, *et al., Sources of Japanese Tradition,* Chapter 29, "Two J's." This translation is included in H. Byron Earhart, *Religion in the Japanese Experience,* p. 114.

III. FOSSILIZATION AND RENEWAL

the Christian and Japanese traditions was the rare exception. For many Japanese Christians the imitation of countless foreign national customs and denominational practices in Japan seemed superfluous. Nevertheless, Christmas became quite popular for many Japanese people, apart from its specific Christian significance. It is still celebrated as a children's festival and enjoys almost the same commercial stimulus as in the West.[3]

Christianity gained most of its followers from the youth who attended Christian schools. Christian missionaries made a great contribution to Japanese education, particularly in girls' schools and in the teaching of foreign languages such as English. Young people were encouraged to attend these schools and thereby came into contact with Christianity which was taught openly or privately. In fact until the late 1880s, the tendency for uncritical acceptance of anything Western, including Christianity, alarmed both the government and the priests of Shinto and Buddhism. However, in the late 1880s, Japan's humiliation by Western powers through unequal treaties was a factor which stimulated reactionary support for Japanese independence from foreign missions. The 1890 Imperial Rescript on Education cleverly removed religious instruction from education on the pretext of religious freedom. In reality, it was a result of the new government policy to counteract Western (and Christian) influence by supporting shrine Shinto and the emperor.

The early Japanese Christians who studied abroad in Europe and the United States were greatly influenced by modern education, movements for women's rights, socialism, and liberal politics. These men played very important roles in shaping the more humane aspects of Meiji government. However, even though Christianity provided the rationale for these social and political reforms, social issues and socialism came increasingly to be conceived apart from Christianity.

Although Japan became committed to Western models in education and industrialization, she could do so without accepting Christianity. Furthermore, well before 1900, several innovations caused strife within Japanese Christianity. Denominationalism became a tragic fact. Theological disagreement between the new liberals and older conservatives further fragmented Japanese Christianity. In addition, the evolutionistic and atheistic philosophies of the West presented live options for many intellectuals. As the government schools equalled and then surpassed the quality of the Christian schools (run by missionaries and Japanese Christians), more Japanese found they could accept Western culture without accepting Western religion. For example, Japanese philosophers are at home with all periods and schools of Western philosophy. While there were some devout Japanese Christians, Christianity did not become a major religion in Japan.

After 1890 the youth came under the influence of nationalistic education and the mood of the country gradually changed from nationalism to ultranationalism.

---

[3]See David W. Plath, "The Japanese Popular Christmas: Coping with Modernity." This article is abridged in H. Byron Earhart, *Religion in the Japanese Experience*, pp. 265–70.

Victories in the Sino-Japanese war of 1894–1895 and the Russo-Japanese war of 1904–1905 greatly increased nationalistic fervor. From this time through 1945 Japan's primary focus was strengthening Japan against the Western powers. People were no longer attracted to Christianity just because it was a foreign religion.

Most Japanese Christians supported all aspects of nationalism and militarism. They, for instance, supported both the Sino-Japanese and Russo-Japanese wars, not only in praying for victory, but also in sending aid for the combat troops. By the time of the Russo-Japanese war some Christian intellectuals had become pacifists, but they were the exceptions. Later in the 1930s Japanese ministers were sent to Manchuria at the request of the Japanese soldiers who were Christians. Statistics of religious affiliation are particularly difficult to determine in Japan, but by the turn of the century there were about 75,000 church members, and by the late 1930s about 300,000 Christians. Because the total population was about 80 million at this time, it represented a lower percentage of total Christians —both Protestant and Roman Catholic—than at the peak of earlier Roman Catholicism in the early seventeenth century. Of course, one can argue that in the sixteenth and seventeenth centuries mass conversions of feudal domains took place, whereas in the nineteenth and twentieth centuries conversions were individual and more sincere. Nevertheless, the total number of prewar church members was less than one percent of the total population. This number is small even when compared with the individual New Religions of the same period.

The New Religions: New Variations from Old Traditions

The term "New Religions" (*shinko shukyo*) has been given to a number of Japanese religious movements which first appeared in late Tokugawa times, gained strength after the Meiji Restoration, and became a dominant force after World War II. The term *shinko shukyo,* literally "newly arisen religions," was first used by journalists, in the implicitly critical tone of newcomers or upstarts. Leaders of the New Religions prefer the more neutral term *shin shukyo,* literally "new religions." However, the term New Religions is misleading because these movements are neither altogether "new" nor are they necessarily complete "religions" in the Western sense. Every New Religion is constituted of elements from one or more of the pre-existing religious traditions: folk religion, Shinto, Buddhism, Confucianism, religious Taoism, and even Christianity. Therefore, these religious movements are as much renovators as innovators, as much renewed religious traditions as new traditions. The later religious movements are often seen as splinters or branches of the main Japanese traditions. (For example, Soka Gakkai, the most powerful and famous of all the New Religions, clearly belongs in the stream of Nichiren Buddhism.) Also, the new movements are not necessarily full-fledged religions, since often they did not break such age-old religious patterns as the Buddhist funeral rites; in other words, the New Religions do not necessarily claim the exclusive attention of the adherents, nor do they necessarily

III. FOSSILIZATION AND RENEWAL

meet all of a person's religious needs. In this sense they may be seen as religious cults or religious societies, rather than independent religions with exclusive claims. Only the Nichiren sect among Japanese traditions (and some New Religions deriving from Nichiren Buddhism) expressed an exclusive claim to absolute truth.

Because the New Religions are so numerous and draw on the whole panorama of Japanese religion, it is difficult to summarize them. In order to understand their emergence, it is necessary to recognize the context of Japanese religion and society from which they sprang. By late Tokugawa times, when the first New Religions appeared, organized religion in Japan had become highly formalistic and stagnant. From late Tokugawa times through the post-Meiji era, social and economic conditions were very depressed for poor farmers and city laborers. Although the Meiji Restoration was brought about partially by peasant revolts, the money economy and tax system of the Meiji era only increased the tendency for small farmers to become helpless tenants. Farmers who became city laborers suffered from low wages and poor working conditions of the early capitalistic system. The New Religions found many of their leaders and members from the depressed classes, people who had suffered together and now shared their religious experiences. The economic and social crises helped stimulate a spiritual renewal of the older traditions in forming special religious movements.

The New Religions got their start in the early nineteenth century, but were not officially recognized as completely independent until 1945. Both the Tokugawa government and the later government maintained a strict control over religious sects. During the Tokugawa period the new religious movements were forced to continue within the traditional forms of Shinto. They continued within varying phases of recognition or suppression until 1882 when state Shinto was separated as a government institution from sect Shinto. Thirteen religious movements were recognized and supervised as religious subdivisions of Shinto. Several of the thirteen sects preserved special Shinto traditions, and were actually sect developments of Shinto. Other sects were organized around elements of folk religion and blendings of Buddhism, Confucianism, and religious Taoism. Their origins are so diverse and their later doctrinal systems so complex that it is difficult to make general statements about them.[4]

One of the distinguishing features of all the New Religions is that a living person usually served as either an organizer or founder (or foundress). In most cases the impetus for organizing a religion came from the charismatic quality of the founder or foundress. The founder was considered as semidivine or divine; his or her utterances became revealed scripture. Even the sect developments of Shinto selected special *kami* from the *Nihongi* and *Kojiki* as objects of worship. The New Religions offered specific objects of faith and appealing forms of worship. They usually promised the solution of all problems through faith and

---

[4]See Daniel C. Holtom, *The National Faith of Japan,* pp. 189–286 for a description of the thirteen "Shinto sects" in prewar times.

worship. Some of the founders were led to their crucial religious experience (or revelation) by a personal crisis which was solved by the new faith. Often the New Religions practiced faith healing, but also promised solution to personal crises such as financial and marital difficulties. It may be argued that no religious movement at any time or place is completely new, and the New Religions of Japan certainly demonstrate continuity with earlier Japanese traditions. The six persistent themes within Japanese religious history can be found in the New Religions, too.[5] On the other hand, a certain amount of originality and uniqueness should be accorded these movements.

An outstanding feature of the New Religions is that they made a direct appeal to individual faith, whereas organized religion in Japan had formerly depended upon family membership along hereditary or geographical lines. Each new movement picked up a spark from one of the old traditions and fanned it into a dynamic spiritual force. For example, in the twentieth century Nichiren Buddhism was revived by a number of sects (such as Soka Gakkai) which placed their trust in the Lotus Sutra and other Nichiren practices. Once a New Religion gained followers it tended to become crystallized into organized forms of scriptures, doctrine, worship, and priesthood.

The New Religions have received much criticism as unrefined, superstitious, and even financially questionable. However, their religious vitality is proven by the number of followers they attracted. Even in prewar Japan, before these religions received their biggest stimulus, many sects could claim from several hundred thousand to several million members.[6] It is remarkable that one of them, Soka Gakkai, could gain millions of members in a few decades, while the total number of Protestant and Catholic Christians had not exceeded a half million members in prewar Japan. These New Religions have represented the greatest possibility for religious renewal up to the present day.

SELECTED READINGS

Earhart, H. Byron. "The Interpretation of the 'New Religions' as Historical Phenomena." Interprets the origin and nature of the New Religions within the context of Japanese religious history.

———. *Religion in the Japanese Experience.* See pp. 205–210 for excerpts from the translation of Gauntlett; see pp. 84–97 for excerpts from Holtom; see pp. 249–54 for the significance of the New Religions.

---

[5]For an analysis of the New Religions in terms of these six persistent themes, see H. Byron Earhart, "The Significance of the 'New Religions' for Understanding Japanese Religion." This article is abridged in H. Byron Earhart, *Religion in the Japanese Experience,* pp. 249–54.

[6]See Daniel C. Holtom, *The National Faith of Japan,* p. 285 for membership figures of the thirteen "Shinto sects" in 1937.

Gauntlett, John Owen, trans. *Kokutai no Hongi: Cardinal Principles of the National Entity of Japan.* A translation of the nationalistic textbook used in public schools after 1938.

Holtom, Daniel C. *The National Faith of Japan.* See pp. 189–286 for a prewar sketch of the thirteen divisions of sect Shinto.

Oguchi, Iichi, and Takagi, Hiroo. "Religion and Social Development." A general discussion of the background of Meiji religion.

Ohata, Kiyoshi, and Ikado, Fujio. "Christianity." A contrast of the ideals of Christianity and the social realities of Japan.

Scheiner, Irwin. *Christian Converts and Social Protest in Meiji Japan.* Discusses the warriors who, after the Meiji Restoration, shifted from Confucianism to Christianity as a personal and social philosophy.

17.

Two New Religions: Tenrikyo and Soka Gakkai

The Many New Religions: Differences and Similarities

Of all the New Religions that have arisen in Japan since the early nineteenth century, Tenrikyo and Soka Gakkai are probably the most important; these two movements may also serve to highlight some striking similarities and contrasting differences. Both are new religious movements, founded and organized outside the established religions; but Tenrikyo has been more closely associated with Shinto, while Soka Gakkai comes out of the Nichiren Buddhist tradition. Both movements arose within the active period of the New Religions, the past century and a half, but at different extremes of this period: Tenrikyo was a pioneer New Religion, the first to succeed as a large scale movement, and served as a model for later movements; Soka Gakkai arose about a century later in the prewar period and flourished only after World War II, yet its rapid success had made it the envy of other groups. Although both groups were deliberately founded, the religious dynamics of their founding is quite different: Tenrikyo is oriented around its foundress, seen as a living *kami* who creates her own sacred scriptures and rites; Soka Gakkai reveres as absolutely powerful Nichiren and the Lotus Sutra which its founder rediscovered, but does not place nearly so much trust in the founder as such. Tenrikyo arose in the countryside and has maintained its strength there while moving into the cities; Soka Gakkai arose in the city and has been strongest among urban people, while making some inroads into the countryside.

A brief look at Tenrikyo and Soka Gakkai reveals a number of important features of New Religions, but it is well to point out some characteristics of the many New Religions that differ from these two major movements. Some New Religions were not founded so decisively by one "founder," but tended to coalesce around distinctive regional traditions; this is the case with several movements originally included among the thirteen members of Sect Shinto. Not all the New Religions can be traced clearly to either Shinto or Buddhist derivation; a number of movements are highly syncretistic. Healing is important for several New Religions, much more important than for Tenrikyo and Soka Gakkai. Some groups are more closely related to the Western tradition, through spiritualism and a spiritualistic interpretation of Western science. Although mission activity is practiced by both Tenrikyo and Soka Gakkai, many groups are active only in

Japan. And, of course, not all the New Religions are so large as Tenrikyo and Soka Gakkai.

What we discover in Tenrikyo and Soka Gakkai, then, is a sampling from the hundreds of active New Religions, but this sampling is too limited to provide the basis for generalizing upon all the New Religions. All these new religious movements share common ground, especially the general thrust toward renewing Japanese religious life. But each movement tended to pick up a glowing ember from the slumbering Japanese tradition, and fan it into a blaze of religious enthusiasm. Once the fire was rekindled, each New Religion used its light to seek out its own path. There are many such fires on the Japanese scene today, and Tenrikyo and Soka Gakkai are but two of the brightest.

Tenrikyo: A Living *Kami* and a Joyous Life

The religious nature of Tenrikyo is reflected in the dramatic founding events of this movement. The foundress of Tenrikyo, Mrs. Nakayama Miki (1798–1887, usually referred to by her given name of Miki), led a rather uneventful life as the wife of a farmer until 1838. Miki's son had been ill, and several times she had called in a popular exorcist to cure him. In premodern Japan illness was usually seen as due to the presence of evil spirits, which were driven out by exorcists. In this case the exorcist (a *yamabushi*) used a woman as a medium; after he put the medium into a trance she would identify the evil spirit to be exorcised. But this time when the exorcist was called to heal Miki's son, the exorcist's regular medium was absent, so Miki herself served as the medium. Miki's trance experience, however, was quite unusual: Instead of the usual brief possession and "diagnosis" of illness, Miki received a divine revelation in the form of permanent possession by a *kami* who claimed to be the true original *kami*. The name of this divinity, Tenri O no Mikoto in Japanese, is usually translated into English as God the Parent by Tenri authorities. (Tenri means heavenly wisdom and O no Mikoto is equivalent to royal divinity.) This divinity spoke through the mouth of Miki a rather new message: This *kami* had only loaned Miki her body, but now he was reclaiming it and demanded that Miki spend the rest of her life spreading this message to men. Her family reluctantly yielded to this demand, and this 1838 event marks the traditional founding of Tenrikyo, the religion of heavenly wisdom: From this point Miki is viewed as a kind of living *kami.*

Quickly Miki's fame as a living *kami* spread, and people came to ask her spiritual help, particularly for protection against smallpox and aid in safe childbirth. Gradually there developed a following of people who had received such religious help from Miki. A carpenter (whose wife had been healed by Miki after childbirth) first built a small worship hall and eventually helped bring the teachings of Miki into a more highly organized form. As Miki attracted a larger following and began to hold religious services she came to the attention of the authorities and was subject to harassment and even arrest; in late Tokugawa times religious organizations were closely supervised, and unrecognized religious movements were subject to prosecution. Nevertheless, Miki persevered in her mission of proclaiming faith in Tenri O no Mikoto and her family spread the message to the surrounding area, as far as Osaka. The earliest worship phrase, Namu Tenri O no Mikoto, is quite similar to the Pure Land phrase Namu Amida Butsu and also the Nichiren phrase Namu Myoho Renge Kyo; *namu* translates roughly as "praise be" or "I put my faith in." Eventually, as her following became larger and as Miki devoted more time to her group (especially after the death of her husband), there emerged all the trappings of an organized religion.

Central to the ethos of this emerging movement was the foundress as a living *kami,* and her life was therefore a kind of divine model. What she wrote was considered revelation, and came to be the scripture of Tenrikyo. The songs she wrote became hymns, and the dance she created was transformed into Tenrikyo liturgy. The gestures she used in the dance became standard ritual gestures. Her scripture indicated a nearby spot as the place where the world and mankind were created (by Izanagi and Izanami); this spot, considered the center of the world, became the site for the main shrine of Tenrikyo. The shrine was built in accordance with Miki's revelation, such that there is a square opening in the roof and a wooden column underneath. The corporate worship and elaborate liturgies which Miki established continue to be performed around this column under the open roof; although these features have assumed a mysterious symbolism within later Tenrikyo, they obviously signifiy a channel for continued communication between Heaven and man.

As Tenrikyo gradually developed into a larger organization around the central figure of Miki, it also developed a kind of ethical philosophy of life based on her teachings. Miki taught that "At the very beginning of the world, God the Parent created mankind out of his earnest desire to make them live a *yokigurashi,* a joyous life. Mankind, however, ignoring the will of God the Parent Who created them to live a life of *yokigurashi* in the truest sense of the word, has come to abuse their minds which were granted to them as their own, and becoming self-willed, come to regard life as a gloomy world."[1] Because man has become self-centered and selfish he is surrounded with gloom, but once he recovers his oneness with God the Parent he once again participates in the joyous creation of the world. The means to this joyous life is faith in God the Parent and "sweeping away" one's evils through the worship services instituted by Miki. From a historical viewpoint we might say that this is a religious reform based on a return to Japanese peasant values: gratitude to the sacredness of the cosmos and ethical obligation to place social good before individual profit. The foundress herself worked hard at manual labor and the menial tasks of farming, and her family successors continue this practice, though on a more occasional and formal basis. For the average member of Tenrikyo much emphasis is placed on voluntary labor for the erection of Tenrikyo buildings, and it is customary for these people to

---

[1] *A Short History of Tenrikyo,* pp. 79–80.

III. FOSSILIZATION AND RENEWAL

spend long periods at the Tenri headquarters in unpaid labor. Many Western visitors to Tenri headquarters are so impressed with the infectious happiness and energetic enthusiasm of these voluntary laborers that they compare the atmosphere of Tenrikyo to the vitality of Christianity in its first century of development.

Because Tenrikyo has been described mainly in terms of its development from the life of the foundress Miki, there is not sufficient space to treat all of Tenrikyo's later organization. The movement was forced to accept supervision from other recognized religious bodies, and was granted relatively independent status as an official sect of Shinto in 1908. By assuming the subordinate role of a Shinto sect, Tenrikyo was thereby able to operate more freely, but only after World War II attained real independence. When the foundress died in early 1887, Tenrikyo had already emerged as a rather well organized religion, such that it suffered no critical shock due to the loss of this charismatic leader. The founding site of this religion (later called the city of Tenri) became a kind of Mecca for pilgrimage, with the model of Miki's life and teaching as the compass for the individual believer. The first religious shrines had been erected and the liturgical lines laid down. Succession in the leadership was taken over by male heads of Mrs. Nakayama's family, called patriarchs. Even at the turn of the century Tenrikyo was so highly organized that it had divisions for training ministers, propagation, and missions, and later these divisions approached the complexity of their counterparts in American denominations. For example, Tenrikyo now boasts a large publishing house, issuing works not only in Japanese but also in other Asian and Western languages. Tenri University is a leading private university with an excellent library. The highly efficient central headquarters at the modern city of Tenri are matched by a large nation-wide network of local branches, and a number of overseas branches.

The success story of Tenrikyo is a good lesson for understanding the dynamic power of the New Religions and their impact on the religious scene. Tenrikyo is firmly rooted in traditional Japanese religion, as evidenced in the revelation to Miki through a kind of shamanistic possession. Centering around the charismatic leadership of Miki and relying on established religion only for government recognition, Tenrikyo developed its own scriptural, liturgical, ecclesiastical, and social forms. Thereby Tenrikyo qualified as the first movement to proceed from individual revelation to large scale religious organization. According to a Tenrikyo publication, already in 1899 "the whole number of the churches was 1,493; that of the missionaries, 18,150; and that of the believers, about 2,000,000."[2]

There is no doubt that Tenrikyo's success encouraged other groups to form, and to look upon Tenrikyo's development as a model for their development. But if Tenrikyo has the distinction of being the pioneer or model New Religion, it is also the first New Religion to become a fully organized, or "established" religion.

---

[2]Ibid., p. 158.

Tenrikyo started with every member as a convert into a rather loose group, but eventually saw second, third, and even fourth generation members participate in a highly elaborate ecclesiastical framework. The fate of many would-be New Religions is rather brief, because they are unable to move from charismatic leadership and the initial group to a fully institutionalized religious organization. Tenrikyo made this transition with relative ease, translating the charisma of Miki into institutional lines of authority and liturgy; compared with other New Religions, Tenrikyo has had rather few groups splitting away from it. Like all larger religious organizations, it has received some criticism for increasing formalism and for pressuring believers financially to support the organizational bureaucracy. Such is the dilemma of all organized religion: how to preserve the founding inspiration and the initial vitality within the channels of permanent institutions.

Soka Gakkai: Faith in the Lotus Sutra and a Happy Life

The nature of Soka Gakkai is best shown through the dynamics of its activities and organization, but a brief look at its historical development is necessary for understanding these dynamics. Makiguchi Tsunesaburo (1871–1944), the founder of Soka Gakkai, was a teacher from Hokkaido who developed a new theory of education or theory of value. Makiguchi contrasted the usual three values of truth, beauty, and goodness, with his three values of beauty, gain, and goodness. For he held that truth is objective and absolute, whereas values are subjective and relative; in other words, truth has to be discovered, but values have to be created. This theory, too complicated for simple summary, was developed out of Makiguchi's work in education, but it took on added significance when he became an active believer in the Nichiren Shoshu branch of Buddhism. This meant, roughly, that the absolute truth was identified with Nichiren and the Lotus Sutra; the values to be created were identified as aspects of the happy life available through this absolute faith.

During the 1930s, Makiguchi and Toda Josei (1900–1958), a teacher in the school where Makiguchi was principal, made the first efforts to propagate their new message. They had attracted only several thousand members by 1941 when World War II began. During World War II the movement was suppressed because Makiguchi and Toda refused to comply with wartime directives ordering unified religious support for the military; this would have compromised the absolute truth of Nichiren and the Lotus Sutra with other Buddhist groups and Shinto. The two leaders were imprisoned. Makiguchi died while in prison, but Toda was released in 1945 shortly before the end of World War II. The original movement was so completely destroyed that it is safe to say that Toda is the second founder. In 1951 he decided to devote all of his time to transform Soka Gakkai from a membership of several thousand families to his goal of 750,000 families before he died; the goal was achieved in 1957. This phenomenal success was due in great part to Toda's organizational ability, for he mobilized a large youth division which enthusiastically converted great numbers. Also he was helped by the close ties he renewed with Nichiren Shoshu. After Toda's 1958 death, his protege Ikeda Daisaku (1928–) became Soka Gakkai's third president (in 1960). Toda's aggressive conversion policies and the violent tactics of his youth division had given Soka Gakkai a bad reputation, which Ikeda attempted to improve. Ikeda favored expansion of membership by peaceful persuasion, and oversaw the development of cultural and political activities within Soka Gakkai. Ikeda has consolidated this movement into a more sophisticated and highly efficient modern organization.

To understand the traditional religious background of this dynamic modern movement we must review the inspiration of Nichiren and its later fate. Nichiren emphasized absolute, exclusive faith in the Lotus Sutra and recitation of faith in the Lotus Sutra through the phrase Namu Myoho Renge Kyo (or Nammyoho Renge Kyo, the form preferred by Soka Gakkai). After the death of Nichiren his followers split into groups which in time turned into hard denominational lines. By the late Tokugawa period, people devoted to Nichiren as a religious model and to the Lotus Sutra as a guide were increasingly frustrated with Nichiren denominations. Therefore they formed voluntary organizations called *ko*. Some of these *ko* eventually developed into New Religions; other New Religions (such as Rissho Koseikai) emphasize faith in the Lotus Sutra, but did not emerge from *ko* organizations. Soka Gakkai is more recent than the early Nichiren-derived New Religions, but is by far the largest, most dynamic, and most efficiently organized. Its ethos is defined by the solution of all personal and societal problems through absolute faith in the Lotus Sutra. Soka Gakkai holds to absoluteness not only in the commitment of the believer, but also in the absolute truth of its message. Therefore, it follows that all other religions are false. Likewise, all personal and cultural values must be dependent on this absolute truth. One positive aspect of this absolute faith in an absolute truth is its promise to solve all personal and cultural problems; one negative aspect is seen in the frequent accusation that, especially during the aggressive conversion campaign of the 1950s, absolute faith in the Lotus Sutra left believers open to *any* means in order to convert people to this absolute truth.

The dynamics of Soka Gakkai can best be seen by the way in which a new member is taken into the organization. The grass roots strength of Soka Gakkai is the small discussion group of twenty to thirty people who meet informally in members' homes to share testimonials and discuss personal problems as well as studying Soka Gakkai doctrine. A nonmember usually makes his first contact with Soka Gakkai when a member who happens to be a friend, relative, or co-worker persuades him to attend a discussion meeting. After several meetings the person may seek to solve his problems in the context of such a group with faith in Nichiren and the Lotus Sutra. But in order to become a member of Soka Gakkai he must formally be admitted into Nichiren Shoshu; this necessitates removing all traces of other religions from his home—throwing out or burning the Shinto and Buddhist elements and images which traditionally were an integral part of most homes. (Christian elements, if present, also are forbidden.) Only then can he go to a Nichiren Shoshu temple for the official conversion rites, when he is given a wooden tablet with the title of the Lotus Sutra carved in it. This is patterned after the one which Nichiren himself made, and is a sacred object to be placed in the now empty family altar. Twice every day, morning and night, the member should recite the title of the Lotus Sutra (Nammyoho Renge Kyo) and passages from it before the sacred object. From this time the member will himself participate in the discussion groups and the many other activities of Soka Gakkai. He also must become active in converting others, and is expected to make a pilgrimage to the head temple of Nichiren Shoshu, Taiseki-ji near Mount Fuji. (Several million members make the trip annually.)

The organizational structure of this lay movement is amazingly effective and tight-knit, with a number of interlocking and overlapping subgroups. On the lowest level, there is an inviolable link between a member and the person who converted him, completely apart from geographic or organizational ties. The member as a part of his family also belongs to the small "unit" of ten or twelve families; five to ten units constitute one "group"; a number of groups make up a "district"; the next structural element is the "chapter," including one to two thousand families; several chapters form a "general chapter"; next comes a "headquarters" followed by a "joint headquarters," which is directly controlled by the leadership of Soka Gakkai. Since 1955 Soka Gakkai also introduced the "block" system of geographical units, with every family belonging to the smallest geographical block, and subsequent larger blocks pyramiding into the inclusion of all Soka Gakkai families. Not only does every family belong to both a "unit" and "block," but every individual also belongs to a division such as men's division, women's division, or youth division.[3] It is also possible for one to take competitive examinations on Soka Gakkai doctrine and achieve the academic rank of instructor, assistant professor, or full professor.

The movement is also well organized into bureaucratic areas. It publishes its own religious materials in Western and Asian languages, has conducted highly successful fund-raising campaigns, and has completed phenomenal building programs in Tokyo and at Taiseki-ji. Its Soka University, which opened in 1971, may be seen as the apex of its organizational and building programs. But most of Soka Gakkai's notoriety comes from its participation in politics. In 1964 Soka Gakkai developed the Komeito (Clean Government Party) as a full-fledged party with a large number of local and national candidates, and has been highly successful in electing candidates. Due to the nature of the Japanese political system, many political offices are filled by voting in the top several candidates out of a large field; Soka Gakkai has been able to judge accurately how many votes will be needed to elect a candidate and then, based on how many votes they can command in that area, put up only as many candidates as they can elect. Komeito is the only

---

[3]See the Organizational Chart in *The Nichiren Shoshu Sokagakkai,* p. 19. A high official of Soka Gakkai has written me that this 1966 publication and the Organizational Chart no longer reflect the actual conditions of the movement.

religiously based party in Japanese history, and has already become a major national force. Komeito and Soka Gakkai have been accused of attempting to gain religious control over the state, which they deny. However, after an incident in 1969 and 1970 when both were charged with suppressing publication of a book critical of Soka Gakkai, there was an investigation in the National Diet;[4] afterward Soka Gakkai officially separated itself from Komeito. Since then Komeito has tended to decline somewhat in strength, and therefore the future development and direction of this political movement are uncertain. But Soka Gakkai has been so efficient in mobilizing such a large number of people that it raises a still unanswered question: What is the motivation behind and the goal for this movement? This question becomes relevant for overseas concern, especially as Soka Gakkai (under the name of Nichiren Shoshu) becomes a larger force in American and European cities.

The Significance of the New Religions: Old Wine in New Bottles

The lesson of Soka Gakkai throws a great deal of light on the New Religions in general. For example, we remember that Tenrikyo moved from charismatic leadership of a living *kami* to a large-scale organization. Soka Gakkai also has had charismatic leadership, but its primary focus has been on the Lotus Sutra; this demonstrates the ability to revive a traditional sacred treasure and develop a large-scale religious organization around it. This is like putting old wine in new bottles: The old wine is Nichiren and his interpretation of the Lotus Sutra, and the new bottle is the lay organization of Soka Gakkai. The "old bottles" of organized religion have tended to break apart under the pressures of modern life, especially in cities where secularism and alienation are high. The dilemma in such a modern situation is whether traditional religion can still speak meaningfully to human lives.

Soka Gakkai has been subjected to more adverse criticism by Western journalists and scholars than any other New Religion, the most serious charge being that it is "fascist," using the cloak of religion to gain control of large masses of people for ulterior purposes. Soka Gakkai, of course, has denied the charge, claiming it is truly democratic, with power flowing from the member to the higher groups, the aim being to enrich the lives of all people (creating value based on the absolute truth). One need not be an advocate of Soka Gakkai to question the more sensational charges that Soka Gakkai is a fascist movement about to gain religious control over the whole country. No single religious group in the past has ever been able to completely control Japan, and it is unlikely that this will happen in the future.

To recognize the ambiguity of Soka Gakkai's organizational structure and use of power is to recognize a more universal truth: the ambiguity of all socioreligious institutions and all forms of power. A more serious question in all

---

[4]This episode is described in Hirotatsu Fujiwara, *I Denounce Soka Gakkai.*

modern cultures—where small communities and folk life give way to large cities, dehumanized work, and impersonal religions—is whether people will be controlled by: 1) nationalism, 2) ideology (apart from national identity), 3) mass media and consumerism, 4) religious commitment. From the Meiji Restoration of 1868 to the end of World War II in 1945, Japan was controlled primarily by nationalism, with religious support from all organized religion, and a primary goal was the development of heavy industry. In fact, Japan's strong national identity probably helped immunize it from the type of ideological control that overtook China. (Communism has had some appeal for intellectuals, but has never been a major political factor in Japan.) After 1945 nationalism has still been present in Japan, particularly as evidenced by increasing military expenditures, but nationalism seems to be secondary to the popular values of acquiring consumer goods. Education is a good indicator of national values, and whereas nationalism in school texts has been toned down considerably in Japan after 1945, the thrust toward consumerism is much more pronounced than in prewar times. (Japan has one of the highest rates of television sets per population in the world, and advertising is highly developed.) Modern countries tend to acculturate the young in school systems where nationalism, political ideology, technological competence (training for a job), and the value of consumer goods are all taught. These factors are all related, and they do contain implicit religious values: as we know in the West, the "Protestant ethic" of hard work has been closely related to the capitalistic system. In Japan, too, economic strength may be the new channel in which nationalism flows, and it may be fed by religious pride for the Japanese tradition. But explicit religious values are weak in this modern setting, and Soka Gakkai has its finger on something important, in that many modern people sense a lack of value in this life style. Viewed in this light, religious values in Japan seem hopelessly outranked by economic and national concerns; indeed, Soka Gakkai claims to be a religious alternative to the dominant materialism of contemporary Japan.

It is not the task of scholars to persuade people to join Soka Gakkai or any other religious organization—this is an existential decision for each individual. But the common predicament for all modern people is life within secular surroundings: Can man find meaning and joy in life by completely secular means? Many modern Japanese have answered "no" to this question. Individually, they have actually embraced one of the many New Religions; in so doing they have affirmed traditional Japanese religious values, but shown also their preference for new ways of organizing and expressing these values.

SELECTED READINGS
Arai, Ken. "New Religious Movements," in *Japanese Religion,* edited by Ichiro Hori, pp. 89–104. A concise overview of the definition and major features of the New Religions.
Blacker, Carmen. "New Religious Cults in Japan." A good first article to read, discussing the origins of the New Religions in folk religion and popular religion.
Earhart, H. Byron. *Religion in the Japanese Experience.* See Part Fifteen for selected

documents on the New Religions, including excerpts from the article by Earhart and the Tenrikyo and Soka Gakkai publications listed below.

———. "The Significance of the New Religions for Understanding Japanese Religion." A general discussion of the New Religions in terms of six persistent themes in Japanese religion.

Ikado, Fujio. "Trend and Problems of New Religions: Religion in Urban Society." A sociological analysis of the relationship between increased urbanization and the expansion of the New Religions in the postwar period.

Murata, Kiyoaki. *Japan's New Buddhism. An Objective Account of Soka Gakkai.* A general introduction based mainly on the publications of Soka Gakkai.

The Nichiren Shoshu Sokagakkai. A publication by this organization about its philosophy of life, activities, and goals.

A Short History of Tenrikyo. Published by Tenrikyo headquarters, it includes chapters on the life of the foundress, the history of the movement, and its activities.

Straelen, Henry van. *The Religion of Divine Wisdom.* The most complete account of Tenrikyo by a Western scholar.

18.

Religion in Postwar Japan

Shinto: Disestablishment and Popular Disfavor

When World War II ended in 1945, a dramatically new age dawned in Japan. For the first time this nation had been defeated, her own soil occupied. This marked a reversal of the nationalistic mood which dominated from 1868 to 1945. Japanese religion still has not fully recovered from the disorientation caused by the defeat and its implications for religious bodies.

The most obvious religious feature of the defeat was the official disestablishment of shrine Shinto by the order of the Allied occupational forces. The emperor announced defeat over the radio. Later he made the announcement that he was not a god but only human.[1] The occupational forces did not intend to change Shinto insofar as it was the religion of the people, but insisted that neither Shinto nor any other religion should be the tool of militaristic nationalism. This clearly indicated the end of Shinto's "nonreligious" status and special role in government. In effect, Shinto shrines throughout the country once more were treated as religious institutions, along with Buddhist temples and Christian churches. Shinto priests ceased being government officials, and government subsidies to shrines stopped. Even more important was the removal of religious nationalism from school textbooks and the mass media.

It is hard to understand what happened in the minds of the Japanese people at the time of defeat and thereafter. Some Westerners, on the basis of the fanatic resistance of Japanese soldiers during the war, predicted that every Japanese town would put up a last-ditch defense. Yet after the emperor's broadcast announcing surrender there was almost no resistance. Even in defeat the emperor's authority commanded obedient respect.

Shinto had profited the most from government support between 1868 and 1945, so of course it suffered the most from the removal of support. Although Shinto suffered from financial loss, even greater was the loss of the people's sympathy. When people lamented the war's destruction they tended to blame Shinto as the tradition most closely allied to the war machine. Another setback was the disorganization of Shinto. Government control of Shinto before World War II was disliked even by the sincere Shinto priests, but at least it welded Shinto

---

[1]See Daniel C. Holtom, *The National Faith of Japan,* pp. 215–18 for a translation of the "Directive for the Disestablishment of State Shinto"; see pp. 219–20 for a translation of the "Imperial Rescript on the Reconstruction of New Japan," including the so-called "renunciation of divinity." These translations can also be found in H. Byron Earhart, *Religion in the Japanese Experience,* pp. 27–34.

together into a national religious force. After the war there was complete religious freedom for the first time, because any religious group was able to organize and qualify for tax exemption as a religious body. Most of the Shinto shrines reorganized as the Association of Shinto Shrines, but the prewar groups of sect Shinto declared their independence from Shinto control. Both the Shinto shrines and the Buddhist temples were divested of much of their land holdings, removing a main source of income.

One of the most delicate problems of the postwar period has been the exact relationship of the emperor to the state and to Shinto. There has been disagreement about what it means for the emperor to be the symbolic head of the state. On the one hand are those few who would like to abolish the emperor even as a symbol; on the other hand are those few who would like to give the emperor a more important role in government. In the middle are the majority who seem to be indifferent or respectful (but not worshipful) toward this national symbol. The rituals of the emperor are considered to be his private cult, but there is the troublesome matter of the considerable expense for the ceremonies. Also, Shinto priests feel that the emperor still should represent the chief priest of Shinto and the nation. A further complication is the problem of state financing for certain shrines, such as Ise, which have traditionally received state funds.

Yasukuni Shrine in Tokyo, which since Meiji times developed into a national shrine for the war dead, has become a problem after 1945. Some people have favored more state support for the shrine, even financial support, seeing the shrine as a harmless patriotic monument, somewhat like the Tomb of the Unknown Soldier in America. Others have feared that explicit state support for Yasukuni Shrine would be the first step toward reviving the unity of state and religion that supported ultranationalism and militarism before and during World War II.

Buddhism: The Continuing Need for Renewal

Although Buddhism had supported the war effort, it did not suffer so much from the stigma of defeat. Nevertheless, it was hard pressed due to the loss of temple lands. Furthermore, Buddhism felt the disorganization which resulted from complete religious freedom. Even after 1868 the lines between main temples and subtemples were strictly maintained, and before World War II the government required all Buddhist temples to maintain strictly defined denominational ties. The Allied Occupation removed such government restrictions. Therefore after 1945 temple affiliations became more flexible, and at a time when landed revenues were lost, Buddhism suffered acute financial problems. These are some of the practical problems, but basically Buddhism had not responded to the earlier symptoms calling for a spiritual renewal. Buddhist priests and temples continued to function in funeral and memorial services for most Japanese, but often without inspiring great religious feeling. Some renewal of Buddhism has taken place through increasing participation by laymen (some of whom are internationally known scholars), and through greater awareness of Buddhism as a pan-Asian or even a worldwide religion. However, by far the greatest interest in Buddhism has been in the Buddhist-inspired New Religions.

Christianity: The Problems of Denominationalism and a Japanese Christianity

Widespread dissatisfaction with Shinto and general indifference towards Buddhism would seemingly have been a great opportunity for Christianity to gain converts. Such was not the case. Christianity continued through the war years, somewhat suppressed by the government, but led by Japanese ministers without the aid of foreign missionaries. Christian churches suffered a greater loss from wartime bombing than Shinto and Buddhism, simply because the majority of Christian churches are found in larger cities. The reentrance of foreign missionaries after the war did not cause a radical change in religious affiliation. Christianity was still at a distinct disadvantage because of denominational splintering, theological disagreement, and the perennial problem of a truly Japanese Christianity. Furthermore, the crisis of defeat forced both Shinto and Buddhism to reconsider their basic foundations, giving them greater strength in meeting Christianity intellectually.

No longer was it a simple choice between native and foreign philosophies of life. Even long before the war Japanese intellectuals had become acquainted with Western agnostic and atheistic philosophies, and the extreme crisis of postwar years pushed some to the materialistic philosophy of Marxism. Immediately after the war there was a serious food shortage, followed by the combined problems of reconstruction and inflation. These conditions did not make the ethical monotheism of Christianity any more attractive to the Japanese than it had been before the war. In postwar Japan it is estimated that Christians represent about one half of one percent out of a total population of about one hundred million. Most of those who made a decision of faith as individuals turned to the New Religions.

The Postwar Boom of New Religions

Whereas Buddhism and Confucianism dominated the Tokugawa period, and Shinto dominated the period from 1868 to 1945, in the postwar period it is the New Religions that have captured the limelight. They had the most to gain from the postwar situation in several respects. First, these movements, more than any other religious tradition, escaped the stigma of association with the disastrous defeat. Although some leaders of the New Religions supported the war effort, several of the groups came into conflict with the government control of religion both before and during the war. The New Religions which had been persecuted during the war emerged almost victorious amidst the sense of complete defeat. The many religions which sprang up after the war expressed an atmosphere of exuberance in rejecting the past, and looked forward with promise to the future.

(Depending on how they are counted, at one time there were at least several hundred postwar New Religions.)

Second, the new movements profited most from the complete religious freedom after World War II. While the New Religions were able to attain complete independence for the first time, the "old" religions of Shinto and Buddhism were forced to compete at the same level because of the loss of land revenues and government support. Several additional reasons can be advanced for the phenomenal success of the new groups in postwar Japan. There was the religious freedom of the newer movements which, because they were new, possessed no commitment to outmoded forms and spoke immediately to the religious needs of postwar Japan. In postwar times, the population shifted from 70 percent rural, 30 percent urban, to 70 percent urban, 30 percent rural; these conditions of great mobility tended to dissolve traditional ties to Shinto and Buddhism, making conversion to a New Religion all the more attractive.[2] At the same time, the New Religions had a thoroughly Japanese character which enabled them to give a Japanese answer to their spiritual problems. The new religious movements reflect all the persistent themes in Japanese religious history. This helps explain how the membership of some postwar New Religions could equal or better the total number of Christians in Japan. Another point of strength was the tendency for the New Religions to be openly syncretistic in character, often taking the best features from Buddhism, Shinto, and even Christianity. A theme emphasized by some of the new movements is the unity of all religion. They not only make universalistic statements about religion, but send missionaries throughout the world to spread their world faith.

There is considerable speculation about the role of the New Religions in the future of Japan. Some people fear the growth and increasing power of these dynamic movements. On the other hand, scholars closer to the scene have begun to suggest that the postwar peak of the New Religions is already past, and that a leveling off is in the process. Indeed, one can note that the New Religions themselves have become institutionalized—they now constitute organized religions like the Buddhist and Shinto groups. They have even formed their own Association of New Religions. Most of the new groups have great financial resources, and impressive headquarters in Tokyo or at religious centers. At the same time, it is worth noting that some of the recent movements are not complete religious organizations. For example, members of many New Religions are still buried in Buddhist ceremonies by Buddhist priests. Therefore, it would be a mistake to think that Buddhism and Shinto are defunct. Japanese history shows many cases where a slumbering tradition was revitalized. It is quite likely that, as time passes, the differences between new and old religions will diminish. The newer movements may become more highly organized and institutionalized; the

---

[2]See Fujio Ikado, "Trend and Problems of New Religions: Religion in Urban Society."

established religions of Buddhism and Shinto may adopt some of the successful activities (such as discussion groups) and organizational forms (such as lay participation) from the New Religions.

SELECTED READINGS

Creemers, Wilhelmus H. M. *Shrine Shinto After World War II.* A detailed study of the status and organization of Shinto, especially the impact of reorganization after World War II.

Dore, Ronald P. *City Life in Japan.* See pp. 291–373 for a description of religious life in postwar Tokyo, as based on survey research and interviews.

Earhart, H. Byron. *Religion in the Japanese Experience.* See pp. 222–31 for excerpts from Dore, and pp. 27–34 for excerpts from Holtom.

Holtom, Daniel C. *Modern Japan and Shinto Nationalism.* See Chapters 7 and 8 for comments on Shinto just after World War II, and the appendices for the directive disestablishing Shinto and the emperor's own "renunciation of divinity."

Kitamori, Kazoh. *Theology of the Pain of God.* Considered the most original Japanese Christian theologian, Kitamori has attempted here a genuinely Japanese theology.

Kiyota, Minoru. "Buddhism in Postwar Japan. A Critical Survey." A critical analysis of postwar Buddhism, contrasted with the success of the New Religions.

McFarland, H. Neill. *The Rush Hour of the Gods. A Study of the New Religious Movements in Japan.* A general account of five New Religions.

Plath, David W. "The Fate of Utopia: Adaptive Tactics in Four Japanese Groups." Considers the impact of modernization upon the quality of human life, and the attempt of four communal groups to achieve utopian alternatives.

Woodard, William P. *The Allied Occupation of Japan and Japanese Religions 1945–1952 and Japanese Religions.* A detailed analysis of religious developments and Allied policy toward religion in the Occupation period.

————. "Study on Religious Juridical Persons Law, Text of the Law No. 126 of 1951." Text and discussion of the new law governing religious bodies in postwar Japan.

19.

The History and Future of Japanese Religion

Fossilization and Renewal in Japanese Religion

From Tokugawa times to the present, Japanese religion has undergone a series of major transformations. In the Tokugawa period Buddhism was an arm of the government, while Confucianism provided the rationale for the state. In the Meiji Restoration Buddhism was disestablished, Confucianism was temporarily abandoned, and Shinto was established. From 1868 until 1945 shrine Shinto and nationalistic religion dominated. In 1945 Shinto was disestablished and all religions were supposed to function on an equal basis. The New Religions first appeared in the late Tokugawa period, gained strength between 1868 and 1945, and tended to dominate after 1945. Naturally, these major transformations of Japanese religion were inseparably connected with economic, social and political changes. However, in the light of Japanese religious history, the transformations mark a distinctive period of that history.

The third period of fossilization and renewal must be understood in the light of the two earlier periods. First, there was the formative period from prehistory to the ninth century when all the major formative traditions (except Christianity) made their appearance. Second, there was the period of development and elaboration from the ninth century to the seventeenth century when the formative traditions interacted to produce the interrelationships and specific branches distinctive of Japanese religion. Third, this development and elaboration tended to stagnate into excessive formalization, which in turn called for a renewal. This brings into question the future of Japanese religion, either in the continuation of the third period or with the emergence of a fourth period. We must not assume that religious history ends in Japan with the third period. Although no one can predict without error, several comments about the future can be made on the basis of the three historical periods.

The most obvious comment is that Japanese religion will continue to undergo transformation. One possible transformation might be the demise of the New Religions, but this seems highly unlikely. Just as Buddhism survived the persecution of the Meiji Restoration and Shinto survived the defeat of World War II, so the New Religions will probably survive the leveling off of postwar times. Already they are so highly institutionalized that they can be called "old religions." One pertinent question is the extent to which the New Religions will approach the status of Shinto and Buddhism. The other side of this question is the extent to which the organized religions of Shinto and Buddhism will approach the style of the New Religions. At any rate, both Shinto and Buddhism are concerned about their future and are actively pursuing policies of renewal. It would be too much to expect a sudden or complete transformation of these age-old traditions, but it would be a mistake to think that they will not undergo change.

Major Features of Japanese Religion

Looking at the long history of religion in Japan, we can now recognize the major features of Japanese religion. Although Japanese religion does not display the present Western religious features of belief in one God, affiliation to one ecclesiastical body, and weekly worship services, it possesses a rich and distinctive religious life. The various beliefs and practices in Japanese religion constitute the interrelated network of a total worldview, which enriches human life by bringing it into contact with a sacred or divine power. The religious forms which mediate this sacred power vary somewhat in terms of different types and in terms of historical change, but the general outlines remain the same.

The most general designation of the sacred or divine power is *kami,* but it also includes Buddha, *bodhisattvas,* the way of heaven (in Taoistic terms), and the Confucian notion of social and cosmic order. All of these terms indicate the divinities or sacred foundation on which the universe rests, according to which man must live his life. Especially within folk religion the sacred power is seen in terms of nature itself and the power of fertility. The notion of *kami* ranges from mythological figures to the emperor and other semidivine persons such as national heroes, founders, priests, charismatic and shamanistic leaders, and even family ancestors.

Each form of sacred power has been worshiped or revered in the manner appropriate to it. Some mythological figures and *bodhisattvas* have remained in the background of the national heritage, while others have formed objects of worship for cults. The emperor was always august and removed from direct approach, while charismatic and shamanistic leaders brought sacred power directly to the people. The way of heaven and Confucian order were vague notions indirectly honored by the whole society, while family ancestors were the object of a specific, concrete veneration in each home.

The channels for mediating sacred power to the people are clearest in the case of organized religion. In Shinto the priest was an intermediary between *kami* and man, for the priest chanted the prayers and performed the rituals by which the presence of the *kami* was invoked. Especially during a festival the Shinto parishioner left his everyday surroundings and visited the sacred confines of a shrine, passing through the sacred gateway (*torii*) and purifying himself in preparation for contact with the *kami.* In Buddhism the priest was an intermediary between Buddhist divinities (Buddhas and *bodhisattvas*) and man, for he recited Buddhist prayers and performed Buddhist rituals. There were regular visits to shrines and temples during annual festivals, and also visits for special purposes. Many festivals at Shinto shrines were part of the seasonal agricultural rhythm of praying for good growth and giving thanks for the harvest, but people also visited shrines to gain a blessing for their specific occupation or individual difficulty. Many people visited Buddhist temples during festivals to gain the blessing of the Buddhist divinity at that temple, and made individual visits at other times for special requests such as healing. However, funeral and memorial masses were usually performed only at the family temple where each family enshrined the ashes or memorial tablets of its deceased.

Outside of organized religion the channels for mediating sacred power were more informal. In the traditional home there were regular observances such as the daily offerings to the *kami* (placed on the *kamidana,* "god-shelf") and to the ancestors (placed in the *butsudan,* Buddhist altar). There were also the many itinerant priests and popular practitioners who both warded off evil forces and granted the protection of benevolent forces. The Taoistic notion of living in conformity with the way of heaven blended with the Japanese notion of appreciating the sacred and aesthetic value of nature. The Confucian sense of social order assured that the human order would conform to the heavenly order.

Just as there were various kinds of sacred power and various channels for mediating sacred power, there were also various techniques and means of expressing sacred power. Sometimes the sacred power and means of expression were almost identical. For example, founders of the New Religions were considered both the *kami* that constituted the sacred power and also, through their writings or statements, the means of expressing it. More often the means of expressing the sacred power was simple and immediate. The many charms issued by shrines and temples, and distributed by wandering religious leaders, conveyed divine protection by token of the sacred name or formula written on it. The inscribed stones and religious statues in villages served to protect the village. The rituals of both organized religion and folk religion served the same purpose of bringing man into contact with sacred power, thereby gaining protection and blessing. The various forms of purification rites helped man free himself from death and defilement in order to renew his life and regain harmony with the sacred basis of life. In general, festivals represented the joyful celebration of temporary direct contact with sacred power.

In addition to these concrete means, there were also more abstract and critical approaches to religious fulfillment. Buddhism in particular included philosophical analyses of the nature of the world and human life. Buddhist writings contained both metaphysical statements about reality, and also critical refutations of competing philosophical systems. Taoistic writings and commentaries provided cosmological and mystical expressions of human destiny, while Confucian writings prescribed the socio-ethical order by which man could conform to cosmological principles.

In the past this network of beliefs and practices has united the Japanese people as having a common destiny. Japanese religion defines the religious foundation and unity of one people, one nation, one land. The people were held together not only by the notion of racial descent from the *kami* who created the Japanese islands, but also by the complex network of beliefs and practices which sustained their corporate life. They oriented their lives toward this sacred power which provided protection against evil and promise of fruitful life. In the passage of time some of these notions changed and some of the traditional religious forms have been called into question. The future of Japanese religion must be understood in terms of the recent transformations and their implications for continuity and innovation.

The Prospect for Japanese Religion

Contemporary Japan presents a complex challenge to religion. Both Shinto and Buddhism developed within an agricultural nation, and were tied to the land by their landed revenue. As the nation has become increasingly industrialized and urbanized, both religions have suffered. The very meaning of Shinto as defined by agricultural rhythms is threatened in an industrial-urban setting. Buddhism is hard hit by the social mobility which has upset its parish system. There is great disparity in the financial condition of individual shrines and temples. Those which depended mainly on government subsidy or land income have fallen on hard times. On the other hand, some temples and shrines still flourish by means of other income. Some temples and shrines receive money by being the centers of still popular cults. The older historical landmarks and those in scenic resort areas draw money from sightseers and vacationers. One might expect that Buddhism and Shinto will organize on the basis of a more dynamic faith, imitating the recent success of the New Religions. However, several decades after 1945 is still too soon to see what the religious leaders are willing and able to do.

Both Shinto and Buddhist leaders are investigating these problems. Shinto scholars especially are probing the meaning of Japanese culture, in the attempt to maintain the Shinto heritage in a modern world. Buddhist scholars have become more active in the worldwide Buddhist movement. The New Religions are Japanese religions at heart, but some are making an earnest bid as world religions. Religious Taoism and Confucianism are inconspicuous survivals within other traditions, popular beliefs, and (for Confucianism) in social values. Folk religion is still important, but severely attenuated due to industrialization and urbanization.

A general dilemma facing the entire religious world, both the older and newer religious groups, is the movement away from religion to more secular interests. By the Tokugawa period, growing cities and expanding commercialism shifted some attention to the glitter of city life. But in the twentieth century industrialism and urbanization experienced unprecedented growth, and secularism became much more pervasive. Religious devotion remained strongest in the countryside, while indifference to organized religion became a fact of city life. To a certain extent the New Religions have capitalized on this indifference, but the New Religions obviously are unable to change the nature of city life. For example, leisure is a problem in any modern city, and the Japanese man in the street is apt to spend most of his idle time in a *pachinko* parlor, a kind of slot machine gallery abundant in any city. Such people have little interest in religion. On the other hand, many intellectuals and writers have gone beyond mere indifference to religion, expressing the pessimistic view of the meaninglessness of life. Japan looks to her novelists as cultural heroes, more so than Americans to their writers, and some of Japan's most respected novelists have committed suicide. If religion represents a positive affirmation of life and the world, secularism at most views life as hedonism; and in the shadow cast by secularism is the "negative ideal" of suicide to defeat meaninglessness. Perhaps this extreme form of secularism represents the most serious challenge to religion, since it rejects any traditional religious answer.

The religious problem in Japan is not so different from the same problem in the West. It is a question of how cultural, spiritual, and religious values can be articulated and perpetuated in the modern world.[1] Here modernity means the total effect of several transformations: wide knowledge of the world outside one's own culture, the influence of science and technology on daily lives, a high degree of urbanization and social mobility. There is no clear solution to this problem in either East or West; it is a universal problem. For Japan this means maintaining her own cultural and religious heritage while contributing to a world culture. It is not simply a matter of making Japanese religion conform to new social and economic conditions. It is a human and spiritual question which asks what it means for a Japanese man to live in the present world. It involves the question of how he relates himself to his national history and to the world at large. It implies the question of how he defines himself in relation to the natural world and to his fellow man. The answering of these questions is the task of the Japanese people. This task presupposes a reassessment of Japanese religion.[2]

As we watch the drama of Japanese religion unfold we encounter the richness of this tradition as well as the serious problems facing it. We come to understand how the Japanese people are proud of their tradition, and we sympathize with their attempt to use the resources of their tradition to face contemporary problems. We sympathize with them, for in the final analysis, all modern people are facing a common problem: the problem of relating one's own religious traditions to contemporary questions. As we study Japanese religion and other religious traditions, not only do we become aware of this common problem, but also we find that the challenge of modernity becomes a creative opportunity. This

---

[1]Masaharu Anesaki was well aware of these problems even before World War II. See his views in *History of Japanese Religion,* pp. 375–409, and in his article "An Oriental Evaluation of Modern Civilization." This article is abridged in H. Byron Earhart, *Religion in the Japanese Experience,* pp. 258–61.

[2]See Robert N. Bellah, ed., *Religion and Progress in Modern Asia* for a discussion of this problem of religion and modernity in terms of the notion of progress. Note especially the remarks of Clifford Geertz, pp. 166–67.

19. The History and Future of Japanese Religion

study affords us the opportunity of understanding ourselves, not just as members of our own Western tradition, but within the worldwide history of man's religious experience. The crucial question is: when we study Japanese religion do we become aware of a profound statement about man and his destiny? To the extent that we can answer that question in the affirmative, we have come to a deeper understanding of ourselves and our world.

SELECTED READINGS

Anesaki, Masaharu. "An Oriental Evaluation of Modern Civilization." An earlier (1928) discussion of the role of religion in modern civilization by the father of the science of religion in Japan.

Bellah, Robert N., ed. *Religion and Progress in Modern Asia.* A discussion of the problem of religion and modernity in terms of "progress."

Earhart, H. Byron. *Religion in the Japanese Experience.* See Part Seventeen for selected documents on the history and future of Japanese religion, including excerpts from Anesaki; see also pp. 222–35 for the problem of religious indifference and secularism.

Kitagawa, Joseph M. *Religion in Japanese History.* See pp. 331–40 for this leading scholar's assessment of the future of Japanese religion.

Annotated Bibliography on Japanese Religion: Selected Works in Western Languages

SPECIAL BIBLIOGRAPHIES ON JAPANESE HISTORY AND RELIGION

Bando, Shojun, et al. *A Bibliography on Japanese Buddhism.* Tokyo: The Cultural Interchange Institute for Buddhist Press, 1958. Exhaustive rather than selective; includes obscure Western language articles and books, classified mainly by sect lines.

Beautrix, Pierre. *Bibliographie du Bouddhisme Zen.* Brussells: Institut Belge des hautes études Bouddhiques, 1969. Arranged topically, it includes English publications and features an author index.

*Earhart, H. Byron. *The New Religions of Japan. A Bibliography of Western-Language Materials.* Tokyo: Sophia University, 1970. Provides a general introduction to the New Religions and a general bibliography, followed by listings for individual New Religions; includes author and topical indexes.

Hall, John Whitney. *Japanese History. New Dimensions of Approach and Understanding.* 2d ed. Washington, D.C.: American Historical Association, 1966. The best bibliographical guide to Japanese history, with balanced treatment of the major problems.

*Herbert, Jean. *Bibliographie due Shinto et des sectes Shintoistes.* Leiden: E. J. Brill, 1968. Includes Japanese and Western-language materials arranged by author, with a subject index in French and Japanese.

Ikado, Fujio, and McGovern, James R., comp. *A Bibliography of Christianity in Japan —Protestantism in English Sources (1859–1959).* Tokyo: Committee on Asian Cultural Studies, International Christian University, 1966. Books, pamphlets, and articles arranged alphabetically by author, with separate indexes by title, author, and subject.

The Journal of Asian Studies. Ann Arbor, 1956–. Annual bibliographical issues provide up-to-date, exhaustive listings by topic.

Kato, Genchi, et al. *A Bibliography of Shinto in Western Languages from the Oldest Times till 1952.* Tokyo: Meiji Jingu Shamusho, 1953. Exhaustive rather than selective; arranged alphabetically by author, with subject index.

Kitagawa, Joseph M. "The Religions of Japan," in *A Reader's Guide to the Great Religions.* Edited by Charles J. Adams. New York: The Free Press, 1965, pp. 161–90. The best single bibliographical work on Japanese religions, with valuable commentary.

*Silberman, Bernard. *Japan and Korea: A Critical Bibliography.* Tucson: The University of Arizona Press, 1962. A general bibliography on Japan; arranged topically, with helpful introductions. (For more recent materials see *The Journal of Asian Studies.*)

*Varley, H. Paul. *A Syllabus of Japanese Civilization.* 2d ed. New York & London: Columbia University Press, 1972. A handy historical and topical guide, with suggested readings; useful for teachers and students.

---

*An asterisk before a listing in the bibliography indicates a book available in paperback edition.

Annotated Bibliography   *131*

SPECIAL DICTIONARIES ON JAPANESE HISTORY AND RELIGION

Basic Terms of Shinto. ("Compiled by Shinto Committee for the IXth International Congress for the History of Religions") Tokyo: Jinja Honcho (The Association of Shinto Shrines), Kokugakuin University, and Institute for Japanese Culture and Classics, 1958. An authoritative and convenient vocabulary of some important Shinto terms.

Goedertier, Joseph M. *A Dictionary of Japanese History.* New York & Tokyo: Walker/ Weatherhill, 1968. A convenient handbook, arranged alphabetically by Japanese terms, with a subject index of Japanese terms.

Japanese-English Buddhist Dictionary. Tokyo: Daito Shuppansha, 1965. A reliable work based on a standard Japanese dictionary, with the terms translated into Roman letters and alphabetized.

Katsumata, Senkichiro (gen. ed.). *Kenkyusha's New Japanese-English Dictionary.* Tokyo: Kenkyusha, 1954. A standard work; because the Japanese words are transliterated into Roman letters and alphabetized, it can be used even by those who do not read Japanese.

Yanagita, Kunio (comp.). *Japanese Folklore Dictionary.* Translated by Masanori Takatsuka. Edited by George K. Brady. "Kentucky microcards, Series A., . . . No. 18." Lexington, Kentucky: University of Kentucky Press, 1958. The microcards are awkward to use, but this standard reference work contains valuable material for anyone who does not read Japanese; arranged alphabetically by Japanese terms.

PERIODICALS FOR JAPANESE HISTORY AND RELIGION

Asian Folklore Studies. Tokyo, 1963–. (Formerly *Folklore Studies,* Peiping, 1942–52, Tokyo, 1953–62.) Covering far eastern folklore in general, it includes articles and monographs on Japanese subjects in German and English.

Bulletin de la Maison Franco-Japonaise. Tokyo, 1927–. In French; detailed monographs of a technical nature.

Contemporary Religions in Japan. Tokyo, 1960–. Short articles on postwar religious developments, especially translated materials concerning the New Religions.

The Eastern Buddhist. Kyoto, 1921–37; new series, 1965–. Articles by Buddhists on popular and scholarly topics.

Japan Christian Quarterly. Tokyo, 1926–. Articles mainly on Protestantism and its missions in Japan.

The Journal of Asian Studies. Ann Arbor, 1956– (formerly *Far Eastern Quarterly*). The leading scholarly journal in English on Asian topics.

Mitteilungen der Deutschen Gesellschaft Für Natur- und Völkerkunde Ostasiens. Tokyo, 1873–. Includes monographs on specialized topics in German.

Monumenta Nipponica. Tokyo, 1938–. Articles, translations, and reviews in German and English.

Transactions of the Asiatic Society of Japan. Tokyo, 1872–. The best general periodical of its kind; with a recent topical index.

HISTORIES AND WORKS ON JAPANESE CULTURE

(For additional references, see Hall, Silberman, and Varley in the Special Bibliographies on Japanese History and Religion.)

*Beardsley, Richard K., Hall, John W., and Ward, Robert E. *Village Japan.* Chicago: The University of Chicago Press, 1959. An intensive study of a small rice-growing community through seven years of joint field work, with separate chapters on aspects of community life. (See Chapter XIV for religion.)

*Befu, Harumi. *Japan. An Anthropological Introduction.* San Francisco: Chandler Publishing Company, 1971. A general introduction to aspects of Japanese culture, with suggested readings and many photographs.

*Benedict, Ruth. *The Chrysanthemum and the Sword.* Boston: Houghton Mifflin Company, 1946 (and later editions). An attempt to examine the distinctively Japanese assumptions about life on the basis of written documents; superseded by recent field work such as Beardsley, *et al.*

Brown, Delmer M. *Nationalism in Japan. An Introductory Historical Analysis.* Berkeley: University of California Press, 1955. A historical study of the complex development of nationalism in Japan.

*de Bary, William Theodore, *et al.* Sources of *Chinese Tradition.* New York: Columbia University Press, 1960. A companion volume to *Sources of Japanese Tradition,* it is a convenient resource for the Chinese background of Japanese culture and religion.

*Dore, R. P. *City Life in Japan. A Study of a Tokyo Ward.* Berkeley and Los Angeles: University of California Press, 1958. A detailed sociological analysis of life in a part of postwar Tokyo, valuable for its firsthand description of all facets of city life.

Fairbank, John K., Reischauer, Edwin O., and Craig, Albert M. *East Asia: The Modern Transformation.* Boston: Houghton Mifflin Company, 1965. The chapters on Japan form a highly respected and widely used text on modern Japanese history (see Reischauer and Fairbank for the first volume of this two volume work).

Hall, John Whitney, and Beardsley, Richard K., ed. *Twelve Doors to Japan.* New York: McGraw Hill Book Company, 1965. Twelve general chapters on topics such as geography, history, personality, art, education, political system, economic development, and law.

*Henderson, Harold G. *An Introduction to Haiku. An Anthology of Poems and Poets from Basho to Shiki.* Garden City, New York: Doubleday & Company, 1958. A sensitive introduction to haiku; a good first book for becoming acquainted with Japanese culture and art.

*Ishida, Takeshi. *Japanese Society.* New York: Random House, 1971. A general introduction to aspects of Japanese society.

*Jansen, Marius B., ed. *Changing Japanese Attitudes Toward Modernization.* Princeton: Princeton University Press, 1965. Articles by leading scholars on specific problems of modernization; this is the first of five volumes on modern Japan published by Princeton University Press (see also Shively).

*Keene, Donald, ed. *Anthology of Japanese Literature from the Earliest Era to the Mid-Nineteenth Century.* New York: Grove Press, 1955. Selected translations from all forms of literature, arranged by historical period.

*_____. *Japanese Literature. An Introduction for Western Readers.* New York: Grove Press, 1955. A concise survey of poetry, theater, and novels.

_____. *Living Japan.* Garden City, New York: Doubleday & Company, 1959. A popular, impressionistic introduction to Japan through many photographs and general discussions.

Maraini, Fosco. *Meeting With Japan.* Translated by Eric Mosbacher. New York: The Viking Press, 1959. A kind of travel book, whose impressions are complemented by many good photographs.

*Munsterberg, Hugo. *The Arts of Japan. An Illustrated History.* Rutland, Vermont: Charles E. Tuttle Company, 1957. A handy one-volume treatment of the various art forms (including folk art), with many illustrations.

*Nakane, Chie. *Japanese Society.* Berkeley and Los Angeles: University of California Press, 1972. A provocative analysis of Japanese society emphasizing its "vertical structure."

Annotated Bibliography 133

Paine, Robert Treat, and Soper, Alexander. *The Art and Architecture of Japan.* Baltimore: Penguin Books, 1955. A scholarly historical analysis divided into painting and sculpture, and architecture, with numerous plates.

*Putzar, Edward. *Japanese Literature. A Historical Outline.* Tucson, Arizona: The University of Arizona Press, 1973. A volume of translated essays by Japanese scholars surveying Japanese literature by historical period; includes a convenient list of translations and studies of Japanese literature.

Reischauer, Edwin O., and Fairbank, John K. *East Asia: The Great Tradition.* Boston: Houghton Mifflin Company, 1958. The chapters on Japan form a highly respected and widely used text on premodern Japanese history (see Fairbank and Reischauer for the second volume of this two volume work).

*_____. *Japan: The Story of a Nation.* New York: Alfred A. Knopf, 1970. A popular presentation by a leading Japanologist, a good first book on Japan.

*Sansom, Sir George. *A History of Japan.* 3 vols. Stanford University Press, 1958–63. A standard Western work, especially valuable for cultural history, covering the span from earliest times until 1867.

_____. *A Short Cultural History.* Revised ed. New York: Appleton-Century-Crofts, 1943. A brief historical treatment of Japanese culture.

*Shively, Donald H., ed. *Tradition and Modernization in Japanese Culture.* Princeton: Princeton University Press, 1971. Articles by leading scholars on specific problems of modernization in Japanese culture; this is the fifth of five volumes on modern Japan published by Princeton University Press (see also Jansen).

Smith, Robert J., and Beardsley, Richard K., ed. *Japanese Culture. Its Development and Characteristics.* Chicago: Aldine Publishing Company, 1962 (Viking Fund Publications in Anthropology, XXXIV). Articles on the origin and nature of Japanese culture by Japanese and Western scholars.

*Thompson, Laurence G. *Chinese Religion: An Introduction.* Encino and Belmont, California: Dickenson Publishing Company, 1969. A brief introduction, helpful for understanding the Chinese background of Japanese religion; includes a bibliography.

*Tsuneishi, Warren M. *Japanese Political Style. An Introduction to the Government and Politics of Modern Japan.* New York and London: Harper & Row, 1966. A convenient introduction emphasizing the peculiarities of the "Japanese political style."

*Tsunoda, Ryusaku, *et al.* *Sources of Japanese Tradition.* New York: Columbia University Press, 1958. A valuable collection of translated documents and comments on Japanese literature, thought, and religion. (See de Bary for the companion *Sources of Chinese Tradition.*)

*Varley, H. Paul. *Japanese Culture. A Short History.* New York: Praeger Publishers, 1973. A concise historical survey of Japanese culture, with numerous photographs.

*Vogel, Ezra F. *Japan's New Middle Class: The Salary Man and His Family in a Tokyo Suburb.* 2d ed. Berkeley and Los Angeles: University of California Press, 1971. The result of extensive field work, it provides an insight into contemporary family life.

Waley, Arthur, trans. *The Tale of Genji.* London: George Allen & Unwin, 1935; several recent editions. Important as the world's first novel, it reveals the court pageantry and religious life of medieval Japan.

Histories and General Works on Japanese Religion

Anesaki, Masaharu. *History of Japanese Religion.* London: Kegan Paul, Trench, Trubner, 1930; reprinted, Rutland, Vermont: Charles E. Tuttle Company, 1963. The standard one-volume history, but somewhat outdated.

_____. "Japanese Mythology," in *The Mythology of All Races.* Edited by Louis H. Gray. Boston: Marshall Jones Company, 1928. Vol. VIII, 207–387, 395–400. A general summary.

———. "An Oriental Evaluation of Modern Civilization," in *Recent Gains in American Civilization.* Edited by Kirby Page. New York: Harcourt, Brace and Company, 1928, pp. 329–57; reprinted in his *Katam Karaniyam. Lectures, Essays and Studies.* Boston: Marshall Jones Company, 1936, pp. 32–51. A stimulating discussion of the role of religion in modern civilization.

———. *Religious Life of the Japanese People.* Revised by Hideo Kishimoto. Tokyo: Kokusai Bunka Shinkokai, 1961. A convenient overview of Japanese religion, with valuable remarks on the turmoil of the prewar and postwar religious situation, and illustrations.

Basabe, Fernando M., Shin, Anzai, and Lanzaco, Federico. *Religious Attitudes of Japanese Men. A Sociological Survey.* Tokyo and Rutland, Vt.: Sophia University and Charles E. Tuttle Company, 1968. An attempt to survey belief and lack of belief by the questionnaire method; includes questionnaires, results, and conclusions.

———, Shin, Anzai, and Nebreda, Alphonso M. *Japanese Youth Confronts Religion. A Sociological Survey.* Tokyo and Rutland, Vt.: Sophia University and Charles E. Tuttle Company, 1967. An attempt to survey religious attitudes by the questionnaire method; includes questionnaires, results, and conclusions. (The two preceding books by Basabe *et al.* are summarized in a popular paperback edition: Basabe, Fernando M. *Japanese Religious Attitudes.* Maryknoll, New York: Orbis Books, 1972.)

Bellah, Robert N., ed. *Religion and Progress in Modern Asia.* New York: The Free Press, 1965. A discussion of the problem of religion and modernity in terms of "progress."

*———. *Tokugawa Religion.* Glencoe, Illinois: The Free Press, 1957. A sociological analysis of a highly eclectic Tokugawa movement; this author argues for the existence of a kind of "Protestant ethic" in Japan.

Bloom, Alfred. "Japan: Religion of a Sacred People in a Sacred Land," in *Religion and Man.* Edited by W. Richard Comstock, pp. 336–94. New York: Harper & Row, 1971 (also in a paperback edition). A concise summary of Shinto and Buddhism.

Clement, Ernest. "Calendar (Japanese)," in *Encyclopaedia of Religion and Ethics.* Edited by James Hastings. III, pp. 114–17. A general picture of the Japanese calendar.

*Earhart, H. Byron. *Religion in the Japanese Experience: Sources and Interpretations.* Encino and Belmont, California: Dickenson Publishing Company, 1974. A convenient sourcebook of brief documents revealing the history and dynamics of Japanese Religion.

———. *A Religious Study of the Mount Haguro Sect of Shugendo. An Example of Japanese Mountain Religion.* Tokyo: Sophia University, 1970. A detailed study of one Shugendo sect, which incorporates influence from most Japanese religious traditions.

———. "Toward a Unified Interpretation of Japanese Religion," in *The History of Religions: Essays on the Problem of Understanding.* Edited by Joseph M. Kitagawa. Chicago: The University of Chicago Press, 1967, pp. 195–225. A discussion of Western scholarship on Japanese religion in terms of the problem of understanding Japanese religion.

Gauntlett, John Owen, trans. *Kokutai no Hongi: Cardinal Principles of the National Entity of Japan.* Cambridge: Harvard University Press, 1949. A translation of t. nationalistic textbook used in public schools after 1938.

Gundert, Wilhelm. *Japanische Religionsgeschichte. Die Religionen der Japaner und Kc reaner in geschichtlichen Abriss dargestellt.* Tokyo: Taiheiyosha, 1935. Photomechanical reproduction, Stuttgart: D. Gundert Verlag, 1943. A standard historical survey.

Hori, Ichiro, ed. *Japanese Religion.* Translated by Yoshiya Abe and David Reid. Tokyo and Palo Alto: Kodansha International, 1972. A volume of essays by Japanese scholars surveying Japanese religious traditions and organizations.

Japan. Ministry of Education. *Religions in Japan.* 2d ed. Tokyo: Government of Japan, 1963. A government publication valuable for its official statistics on organized religious bodies.

Kidder, J. E., Jr. *Japan Before Buddhism.* Revised ed. London: Thames and Hudson, 1966. The best single book on prehistoric Japan, with discussions of the religious implications of the diverse archaeological evidence.

Kishimoto, Hideo. "The Meaning of Religion to the Japanese People," in *Religious Studies in Japan.* Tokyo: Maruzen Company Ltd., 1959, pp. 22–28. A good contrast of Japanese religion with religion in Western civilization.

———, and Wakimoto, Tsuneya. "Introduction: Religion During Tokugawa," in *Japanese Religion in the Meiji Era.* Edited by Hideo Kishimoto. Translated by John F. Howes. Tokyo: Obunsha, 1956, pp. 3–33. This overview of religion in the Tokugawa period illustrates a critical approach to Japanese religion.

Kitagawa, Joseph M. "Prehistoric Background of Japanese Religion," *History of Religions,* II (1963), 292–328. A good summary of Japanese and Western scholarship on the earliest Japanese religion.

———. *Religion in Japanese History.* New York: Columbia University Press, 1966. The most complete, up-to-date account of Japanese religion in a single volume, it combines Japanese and Western materials with the recent insights of the study of religion.

*———. "Religions of Japan." In *The Great Asian Religions.* Compiled by Wing-tsit Chan, *et al.,* pp. 231–305. London: The Macmillan Company, 1969. Translated documents concerning Japanese religion, from early mythology to the New Religions.

Lay, Arthur Hyde. "Japanese Funeral Rites," *Transactions of the Asiatic Society of Japan,* XIX (1891), 507–44. A general survey of funeral rites from the archaeological evidence in prehistoric times through various transformations up to recent times, it includes both Buddhist and Shinto practices.

Morioka, Kiyomi and Newell, William H., ed. *The Sociology of Japanese Religion.* Leiden: E. J. Brill, 1968 *(Journal of Asian and African Studies,* III, Nos. 1, 2; 1968). Short scholarly articles featuring sociological analysis of folk religion, Buddhism, Christianity, and the New Religions.

Munro, Neil Gordon. *Ainu Creed and Cult.* London: Routledge & Kegan Paul, 1962. A descriptive work based on field work earlier in this century, it includes numerous photographs.

*Nakamura, Hajime. *Ways of Thiking of Eastern Peoples: India, China, Tibet, Japan.* Hololulu: East-West Center Press, 1964, revised English translation, edited by Philip P. Wiener. An attempt to describe the peculiarity of the Japanese people through the thought patterns which define this culture.

Norbeck, Edward. *Religion and Society in Modern Japan: Continuity and Change.* Houston: Tourmaline Press, 1970. A treatment of modern Japanese religion as a functional response to social and economic change.

Numazawa, Franz Kiichi. "Die Religionen Japans," in *Christus und die Religionen der Erde.* Edited by Franz Konig. Freiburg: Verlag Herder, 1959. Band III, 393–436. An interesting interpretation by a Japanese ethnologist and Catholic priest.

Oguchi, Iichi, and Takagi, Hiroo. "Religion and Social Development," in *Japanese Religion in the Meiji Era.* Edited by Hideo Kishimoto. Translated by John F. Howes. Tokyo: Obunsha, 1956. pp. 311–57. Interprets the background of Meiji religion, as determined by social and economic factors.

Ooms, Herman. "The Religion of the Household: A Case Study of Ancestor Worship in Japan," *Contemporary Religions in Japan,* VIII, Nos 3–4 (September–December 1967), pp. 201–333. A detailed description of field work in a village near Tokyo, including theoretical considerations.

Piovesana, Gino K. *Recent Japanese Philosophical Thought 1862–1962. A Survey.* Tokyo: Enderle Bookstore, 1963. A survey of the broad range of Western philosophy among Japanese philosophers.

Plath, David W. "Where the Family of God Is the Family: The Role of the Dead in Japanese Households," *American Anthropologist,* LXVI, No. 2 (April 1964), pp. 300–317. Criticism of the older notion of ancestor worship, and suggestion of its replacement with the three categories of the departed, ancestors, and outsiders.

Religious Studies in Japan. Edited by Japanese Association for Religious Studies. Tokyo: Maruzen, 1959. Excellent short articles by the leading Japanese authorities.

Revon, Michel. "Ancestor-Worship and Cult of the Dead (Japanese)," *Encyclopaedia of Religion and Ethics.* Edited by James Hastings. I, 455–57. An interesting early discussion of the controversy concering "ancestor worship" and "nature worship" in Japan. (Many of the articles concerning Japanese religion in this encyclopedia are outdated.)

Sansom, Sir George. "Early Japanese Law and Administration," *Transactions of the Asiatic Society of Japan,* Second Series, IX (1932), 67–109, XI (1935), 117–49. Includes a description of the governmental department of religion in ancient Japan.

Woodard, William P. *The Allied Occupation of Japan 1945–1952 and Japanese Religions.* Leiden: E. J. Brill, 1972. A detailed analysis of religious developments and the Allied policy toward religion in the Occupation period.

――――. "Study on Religious Juridical Persons Law, Text of the Law No. 126 of 1951," *Contemporary Japan,* XXV, No. 3 (1958), 418–70; XXV, No. 4 (1959), 635–57; XXVI, No. 1 (1959), 96–115; XXVI, No. 2 (1959), 239–312. Text and discussion of the new law governing religious bodies in postwar Japan.

SHINTO

*Aston, W. G., trans. *Nihongi. Chronicles of Japan from the Earliest Times to* A.D. *697.* Originally published in *Transactions of the Japan Society,* Supplement I, London, 1896; reprinted, two volumes in one with original pagination. London: George Allen & Unwin, 1956. Covers the same period as the *Kojiki,* but it adds other tales, adopts a Chinese style of writing, and continues the chronology to 697 A.D.

Bock, Felicia Gressitt, trans. *Engi-Shiki: Procedures of the Engi Era, Books I–V.* Tokyo: Sophia University, 1970. A translation of eighth century government regulations concerning Shinto shrines, their administration, and rituals; includes introductory chapters on early Shinto.

――――, trans. *Engi-Shiki: Procedures of the Engi Era, Books VI–X.* Tokyo: Sophia University, 1972. Continuation of the preceding work.

*Bownas, G. "Shinto," in *The Concise Encylopedia of Living Faiths.* Edited by R. C. Zaehner. Boston: Beacon Press, 1967, pp. 348–64. A good brief discussion of early Shinto in terms of purification from pollution.

Chamberlain, Basil Hall, trans. *"Ko-ji-ki, or Records of Ancient Matters,"* *Transactions of the Asiatic Society of Japan,* X, Supplement (1882). The oldest written record in Japan, it is a combination of mythology and court chronology to about the end of the fifth century A.D., preserving the older language and traditions.

Creemers, Wilhelmus H. M. *Shrine Shinto After World War II.* Leiden: E. J. Brill, 1968. A detailed study of the status and organization of Shinto, especially the impact of reorganization after World War II.

Ellwood, Robert S. *The Feast of Kingship. Accession Ceremonies in Ancient Japan.* Tokyo: Sophia University, 1973. A detailed study of Shinto rituals for the emperor's accession; also includes the general Shinto background of the rituals.

Fridell, Wilbur M. *Japanese Shrine Mergers 1906–12. State Shinto Moves to the Grassroots.* Tokyo: Sophia University, 1973. A detailed analysis of state Shinto in terms of shrine mergers—the general policies, their implementation, and overall results.

Holtom, Daniel C. "The Meaning of Kami," *Monumenta Nipponica,* III (1940), 1–27, 32–53; IV (1941), 25–68. An attempt to interpret the Japanese term *kami* through the Melanesian term *mana.*

———. *Modern Japan and Shinto Nationalism. A Study of Present-day Trends in Japanese Religions.* revised ed. Chicago: The University of Chicago Press, 1947; reprinted, New York: Paragon Reprint Corp., 1963. A good historical treatment of nationalistic Shinto, including chapters on the accommodation of Christianity and Buddhism to Japanese nationalism.

———. *The National Faith of Japan. A Study in Modern Shinto.* New York: E. P. Dutton, 1938; reprinted, New York: Paragon Book Reprint Corp., 1965. Important for its historical information on Shinto; the viewpoint is often questionable.

Hori, Ichiro, and Toda, Yoshio. "Shinto," in *Japanese Religion in the Meiji Era.* Edited by Hideo Kishimoto. Translated by John F. Howes. Tokyo: Obunsha, 1956, pp. 35–98. A balanced treatment of Shinto in the Meiji period.

Institute for Japanese Culture and Classics, Kokugakuin University. *Proceedings, The Second International Conference for Shinto Studies.* Tokyo: Kokugakuin University, 1968. Collected papers by Japanese and Western scholars from a conference dealing with continuity and change in Shinto.

Kato, Genchi. "The Theological System of Urabe no Kanetomo," *Transactions of the Japan Society of London,* XXVIII (1931), 143–50. An excellent treatment of the Shinto theologian Kanetomo, emphasizing his significance for later Shinto thinkers.

———, and Hoshino, Hikoshiro, trans. *Kogoshui. Gleanings from Ancient Stories.* 2d ed., rev. Tokyo: Meiji Japan Society, 1925. Written about 807 A.D., it records a rivalry between several Shinto priestly families.

The Manyoshu. Translated by the Japan Society for the Promotion of Scientific Research. Tokyo: Iwanami Shoten, 1940; reprinted, New York: Columbia University Press, 1965. Compiled in the eighth century, it is an invaluable source of ancient Japanese poetry and religion.

Matsumoto, Shigeru. *Motoori Norinaga: 1730–1801.* Cambridge: Harvard University Press, 1970. A detailed biographical study of the foremost scholar and proponent of Restoration Shinto.

Mizoguchi, Komazo. "Orientation in the Study of Shintoism," in *A Guide to Japanese Studies.* Tokyo: Kokusai Bunka Shinkokai, 1937, pp. 137–53. A prewar appeal for a historical-scientific study of Shinto. Other articles in this prewar volume, and other works published by Kokusai Bunka Shinkokai (The Society for International Cultural Relations) are valuable.

Muraoka, Tsunetsugu. *Studies in Shinto Thought.* Translated by Delmer M. Brown and James T. Araki. Tokyo: Ministry of Education, 1964. Scholarly articles on the nature of Shinto, with close attention to major proponents of Shinto thought systems.

Ono, Sokyo. *Shinto: The Kami Way.* Tokyo: Bridgeway Press, 1962. A systematic or "theological" interpretation of Shinto by a contemporary Shinto scholar.

Phillipi, Donald L., trans. *Kojiki.* Tokyo: University of Tokyo Press, 1968. A recent translation emphasizing linguistic accuracy.

———, trans. *Norito. A New Translation of the Ancient Japanese Ritual Prayers.* Tokyo: The Institute for Japanese Culture and Classics, Kokugakuin University, 1959. The most recent scholarly translation of the *norito,* with brief notes.

Ponsonby-Fane, R. A. B. *Studies in Shinto and Shrines.* Revised ed. Kamikamo, Kyoto: The Ponsonby Memorial Society, 1953. Collected articles of a highly technical nature by a life-long student of Shinto. This is the first volume of the six volume series of Ponsonby-Fane's works, all of which contain valuable detailed articles.

Satow, Sir Ernest, and Florenz, Karl. "Ancient Japanese Rituals," *Transactions of the*

Asiatic Society, Reprints, Vol. II (1927). An older translation of *norito* (ritual prayers) with illustrations and commentary on their religious significance.

Ueda, Kenji. "Shinto," in *Japanese Religion.* Edited by Ichiro Hori. Translated by Yoshiya Abe and David Reid. Tokyo and Palo Alto: Kodansha International, 1972, pp. 29–45. A concise overview of the aspects and dynamics of Shinto.

BUDDHISM

Anesaki, Masaharu. *Nichiren the Buddhist Prophet.* Cambridge: Harvard University Press, 1916. Still the standard work, a study from the viewpoint of religious psychology.

Bloom, Alfred. *Shinran's Gospel of Pure Grace.* Tucson: The University of Arizona Press, 1965. A recent study of Shinran's thought.

Coates, Harper Havelock, and Ishizuka, Ryugaku. *Honen the Buddhist Saint. His Life and Teaching.* Kyoto: Chion-in, 1925; several later reprintings. A careful study of Honen which is valuable for its wider treatment of Buddhism.

de Bary, William Theodore, et al. The Buddhist Tradition in India, China, & Japan. New York: The Modern Library, 1969. A convenient anthology of translated texts (the materials on Japanese Buddhism are taken from *Sources of Japanese Tradition*).

de Visser, Marinus Willem. *Ancient Buddhism in Japan. Sutras and Ceremonies in Use in the Seventh and Eighth Centuries* A.D. *and Their History in Later Times.* 2 vols. Leiden: E. J. Brill, 1935. Difficult reading, but the most authoritative Western reference.

*Dumoulin, Heinrich. *A History of Zen Buddhism.* Translated by Paul Peachey. New York: Pantheon Books, 1963. The best historical treatment of Zen, with a balanced consideration of the relationship between the history of Zen and the "essence" of Zen.

Eliot, Sir Charles. *Japanese Buddhism.* London: Edward Arnold, 1935; reprinted, London: Routledge & Kegan Paul, 1959. Still the standard handbook, it emphasizes continuity with Indian and Chinese Buddhism.

Hakeda, Yoshito S., trans. *Kukai: Major Works.* New York: Columbia University Press, 1972. A scholarly introduction to the life and thought of the founder of Shingon Buddhism, with translations of his works.

Hanayama, Shinsho, et al. "Buddhism in Japan," in *The Path of the Buddha.* Edited by Kenneth W. Morgan. New York: The Ronald Press Company, 1956, pp. 307–63. A short treatment by leading Japanese scholars.

―――. "Orientation in the Study of Japanese Buddhism," in *A Guide to Japanese Studies.* Tokyo: Kokusai Bunka Shinkokai, 1937, pp. 87–135. In contrast to Buddhism in Japan, he emphasizes the uniquely Japanese character of *Japanese* Buddhism.

Hurvitz, Leon Nahum. *Chih-i (538–597); An Introduction to the Life and Ideas of a Chinese Buddhist Monk.* Brussels: Institut Belge des hautes études chinoises, 1962. A detailed account of the founder of T'ien-t'ai (Tendai) Buddhism.

Kamstra, J. H. *Encounter or Syncretism. The Initial Growth of Japanese Buddhism.* Leiden: E. J. Brill, 1967. A technical study of the introduction of Buddhism into Japan, and its interrelationships with Chinese, Korean, and Japanese culture.

*Kapleau, Philip. *The Three Pillars of Zen. Teaching, Practice, and Enlightenment.* Boston: Beacon Press, 1967. Interprets the nature of Zen practice and its significance for modern man; includes autobiographical accounts by modern practitioners of Zen.

Kitagawa, Joseph M. "The Buddhist Transformation in Japan," *History of Religions,* IV (1965), pp. 319–36. His division of Buddhism into national Buddhism and folk Buddhism is very suggestive of the religious situation in Japanese history.

―――. "Master and Saviour," in *Studies of Esoteric Buddhism and Tantrism. In Commemoration of the 1,150th Anniversary of the founding of Koyasan.* Koyasan,

Japan: Koyasan University, 1965, pp. 1–26. A valuable biography of Kobo Daishi, emphasizing his significance for popular religion.

Kiyota, Minoru. "Buddhism in Postwar Japan. A Critical Survey," *Monumenta Nipponica*, XXIV, Nos. 1–2 (1969), pp. 113–36. Analyzes the shortcomings of postwar Buddhism by reference to the success of New Religions such as Soka Gakkai.

―――. "Presuppositions to the Understanding of Japanese Buddhist Thought," *Monumenta Nipponica*, XXII, Nos. 3–4 (1967), pp. 251–59. A technical treatment of Japanese Buddhist thought in relation to Mahayana philosophy. (See also Kiyota's forthcoming book on Japanese Buddhism.)

Masunaga, Reiho. *The Soto Approach to Zen*. Tokyo: Layman Buddhist Society Press, 1958. A popular treatment by a leading scholar.

Masutani, Fumio, and Undo, Yoshimichi. "Buddhism," in *Japanese Religion in the Meiji Era*. Edited by Hideo Kishimoto. Translated by John F. Howes. Tokyo: Obunsha, 1956, pp. 99–169. A balanced treatment of Buddhism in the Meiji period.

Matsunaga, Alicia. *The Buddhist Philosophy of Assimilation. The Historical Development of the Honji-Suijaku Theory*. Tokyo and Rutland, Vt.: Sophia University and Charles E. Tuttle Company, 1969. Interprets the interaction between aspects of Buddhism and aspects of Japanese culture.

*Robinson, Richard H. *The Buddhist Religion*. Encino and Belmont, California: Dickenson Publishing Company, 1970. A brief survey of Buddhism, its philosophical and religious developments, and geographical expansion; includes a bibliography.

*Saunders, E. Dale. *Buddhism in Japan. With an Outline of Its Origins in India*. Philadelphia: University of Pennsylvania Press, 1964. A general survey emphasizing the significance of esoteric Buddhism.

―――. *Mudra. A Study of Symbolic Gestures in Japanese Buddhist Sculpture*. New York: Pantheon Books, 1960. A detailed study of the artistic expression of esoteric Buddhism (and Buddhist sculpture in general), with profuse illustrations.

*Suzuki, D. T. *Zen and Japanese Culture*. New York: Pantheon, 1959. Perceptive essays on the Zen penetration of Japanese culture by the foremost Zen spokesman. (Many of Suzuki's works are in paperback editions.)

Tajima, Ryujun. *Les deux grands mandalas et la doctrine de l'esoterisme Shingon*. Tokyo: Maison Franco-Japonaise; Paris: Presses Universitaires de France, 1959. The authoritative work on Shingon doctrine in a Western language, by a late Shingon archbishop.

Takakusu, Junjiro. *The Essentials of Buddhist Philosophy*. Edited by W. T. Chan and Charles A. Moore. Honolulu: University of Hawaii, 1947. Brief analyses of Buddhist philosophical schools.

Tamaru, Noriyoshi. "Buddhism," in *Japanese Religion*. Edited by Ichiro Hori. Translated by Yoshiya Abe and David Reid. Tokyo and Palo Alto: Kodansha International, 1972, pp. 47–69. A concise overview of the origin and historical development of Japanese Buddhism.

*Tsukamoto, Zenryu. "Japanese and Chinese Buddhism," in *Religions and the Promise of the Twentieth Century*. Edited by Guy S. Metraux and Francois Crouzet. New York: The New American Library, 1965, pp. 229–44. A famous Buddhist scholar's critical analysis of the stagnation of "formalized Buddhism" in Tokugawa times and the resulting dilemma for contemporary Buddhism.

Ui, Hakuju. "A Study of Japanese Tendai Buddhism," in *Philosophical Studies of Japan*, Vol. I, pp. 33–74. Compiled by Japanese National Commission for UNESCO. Tokyo: Japan Society for the Promotion of Science, 1959. A detailed analysis of Tendai doctrine, comparing its Chinese origins with its Japanese developments.

*Watanabe, Shoko. *Japanese Buddhism—A Critical Appraisal*. Translated by Alfred

Bloom. Tokyo: Kokusai Bunka Shinkokai, 1964. A frank analysis of "the strong and weak points of Japanese Buddhism" by a Buddhist priest.

CONFUCIANISM

*Hall, John Whitney. "The Confucian Teacher in Tokugawa Japan," in *Confucianism in Action*. Edited by David S. Nivison and Arthur F. Wright. Stanford: Stanford University Press, 1959, pp. 268–301. Describes the Confucian contribution to Tokugawa Japan and its relationship to Shinto and Buddhism.

Smith, Warren W., Jr. *Confucianism in Modern Japan. A Study of Conservatism in Japanese Intellectual History*. Tokyo: The Hokuseido Press, 1959. A good treatment of Confucianism's (Neo-Confucianism's) cultural impact in Japan from 1600 through postwar times.

Spae, Joseph John. *Ito Jinsai. A Philosopher, Educator and Sinologist of the Tokugawa Period*. Monograph XII, *Monumenta Serica. Journal of Oriental Studies of the Catholic University of Peiping*, 1948. Reprinted, New York: Paragon Reprint Corp., 1967. A detailed study of one Confucian thinker, especially valuable for the long first chapter, "Historical Notes on Confucianism in Japan."

Tomikura, Mitsuo. "Confucianism," in *Japanese Religion*. Edited by Ichiro Hori. Translated by Yoshiya Abe and David Reid. Tokyo and Palo Alto: Kodansha International, 1972, pp. 105–22. A concise overview of the role of Confucianism in Japanese thought and society.

RELIGIOUS TAOISM

Frank, Bernard. "Kata-imi et Kata-tagae. Étude sur les Interdits de direction a l'époque Heian," *Bulletin de la Maison Franco-Japonaise*, Nouvelle Série, Tome V, no. 2–4 (1958), pp. 1–246. The only lengthy treatment of the problem, but concerned mainly with the influence of religious Taoism upon medieval literature.

Kubo, Noritada. "Introduction of Taoism to Japan," in *Religious Studies in Japan*. Tokyo: Maruzen, 1959, pp. 457–65. A good summary of an important Taoistic cult.

Miller, Alan L. "Ritsuryo Japan: The State as Liturgical Community," *History of Religions*, XI (1971), pp. 98–124. Includes descriptions of the Bureau of Yin and Yang (Onmyo-ryo) in early Japan.

Saunders, E. Dale. "Koshin; An Example of Taoist Ideas in Japan," in *Proceedings of the IXth International Congress for the History of Religions*, pp. 423–32. Tokyo: Maruzen, 1960. Analyzes the history of Koshin and its dynamics as a Taoist cult.

FOLK RELIGION

Bownas, Geoffrey. *Japanese Rainmaking and Other Folk Practices*. London: George Allen & Unwin, 1963. Popular descriptions of folk religion and customs.

Casal, U. A. *The Five Sacred Festivals of Ancient Japan. Their Symbolism & Historical Development*. Tokyo: Sophia University and Charles E. Tuttle Company, 1967. A colorful description of the major annual Japanese festivals, showing the interpenetration of Buddhism and Shinto in folk religion.

*Dorson, Richard M. *Folk Legends of Japan*. Rutland, Vermont: Charles E. Tuttle Company, 1962. A topical collection, with brief introductions for each tale.

———, (gen. ed.). *Studies in Japanese Folklore*. Chief translator, Yasuyo Ishiwara. Bloomington, Indiana: Indiana University Press, 1963. Translated articles by leading Japanese folklorists, with a helpful introductory chapter on Japanese folklore by the editor.

Earhart, H. Byron. "The Celebration of *Haru-yama* (Spring Mountain): An Example of

Folk Religious Practices in Contemporary Japan," *Asian Folklore Studies,* XXVII, No. 1 (1968), pp. 1–18. Description of a mountain pilgrimage celebrating the coming of spring.

———. "Four Ritual Periods of Haguro Shugendo in Northeastern Japan," *History of Religions,* V (1965), 93–113. Description of the ritual year in an eclectic religious movement.

*Embree, John F. *Suye Mura.* Chicago: The University of Chicago Press, 1939. The pioneer "village study" in Japan; Chapter VII "Religions" demonstrates the interrelationships among the several religious traditions. See the more recent Beardsley *et al., Village Japan* (Chapter XIV), listed above in Histories and Works on Japanese Culture.

Fairchild, William P. "Shamanism in Japan," *Folklore Studies,* XXI (1962), pp. 1–122. Provides considerable information on Japanese shamanism, loosely defined and organized.

Hori, Ichiro. *Folk Religion in Japan. Continuity and Change.* Edited by Joseph M. Kitagawa and Alan L. Miller. Chicago and London: The University of Chicago Press, 1968. Essays showing the complex make-up of folk religion and its importance for understanding Japanese religion.

———. "On the Concept of *Hijiri* (Holy-man)," *Numen,* V (1958), Fasc. 2, 128–60; Fasc. 3, 199–232. Describes the wandering religious figures called *hijiri,* who accepted the religious influences of Shinto and religious Taoism as well as Buddhism and Shugendo.

Miyake, Hitoshi. "Folk Religion," in *Japanese Religion.* Edited by Ichiro Hori. Translated by Yoshiya Abe and David Reid. Tokyo and Palo Alto: Kodansha International, 1972, pp. 121–43. A concise analysis of folk religion, describing its annual festivals, rites of passage, and social organization.

Oto, Tokihiko. *Folklore in Japanese Life and Customs.* Tokyo: Kokusai Bunka Shinkokai, 1963. Although the section on religious activities is rather brief, the book is profusely illustrated with excellent drawings and photographs.

Ouwehand, C. *Namazu-e and Their Themes. An Intrepretative Approach to Some Aspects of Japanese Folk Religion.* Leiden: E. J. Brill, 1964. The most thorough and systematic treatment of Japanese folk religion in English, important for its holistic interpretation.

*Seki, Keigo, ed. *Folktales of Japan.* Translated by Robert J. Adams. Chicago: The University of Chicago Press, 1963. A representative collection, featuring a scholarly foreword and comparative remarks on each tale.

CHRISTIANITY

Boxer, C. R. *The Christian Century in Japan 1549–1650.* Berkeley: University of California Press, 1951. Revised ed., 1967. The authoritative work on early Roman Catholicism.

*Drummond, Richard H. *A History of Christianity in Japan.* Grand Rapids, Michigan: William B. Eerdmans Publishing Company, 1971. A convenient one-volume history, covering the entire span of Catholic, Protestant, and Orthodox developments.

Germany, Charles H. *Protestant Theologies in Modern Japan.* Tokyo: IISR Press, 1965. A survey of the broad range of Protestant theology among Japanese theologians.

Iglehart, Charles W. *A Century of Protestant Christianity in Japan.* Rutland, Vermont: Charles E. Tuttle Company, 1959. A standard historical treatment of Protestantism in Japan.

Kitamori, Kazoh. *Theology of the Pain of God.* Richmond, Virginia: John Knox Press, 1965. Kitamori, hailed as the first original theological writer in Japan, has here attempted a genuinely Japanese theology.

*Laures, Johannes. *The Catholic Church in Japan. A Short History.* Rutland, Vermont: Charles E. Tuttle Company, 1954. A popular work by a recognized authority.

Ohata, Kiyoshi and Ikado, Fujio. "Christianity," in *Japanese Religion in the Meiji Era.* Edited by Hideo Kishimoto. Translated by John F. Howes. Tokyo: Obunsha, 1956, pp. 171–309. A historical treatment by two Japanese Christians, emphasizing the ideals of Christianity and the social realities of Japan.

Plath, David W. "The Japanese Popular Christmas: Coping with Modernity," *Journal of America Folklore,* LXXVI (1963), 309–17. An interesting description of the widespread celebration of Christmas in Japan.

Scheiner, Irwin. *Christian Converts and Social Protest in Meiji Japan.* Berkeley and Los Angeles: University of California Press, 1970. Examines the relationship between *samurai* ideals and Christian ethics in the lives of *samurai* converts to Christianity.

Suzuki, Norihisa. "Christianity," in *Japanese Religion.* Edited by Ichiro Hori. Translated by Yoshiya Abe and David Reid. Tokyo and Palo Alto: Kodansha International, 1972, pp. 71–87. A concise overview of the "foreignness" of Christianity in Japan and its major developments.

NEW RELIGIONS

Arai, Ken. "New Religious Movements," in *Japanese Religion.* Edited by Ichiro Hori. Translated by Yoshiya Abe and David Reid. Tokyo and Palo Alto: Kodansha International, 1972, pp. 89–104. A concise overview of the definition and major features of the New Religions.

Blacker, Carmen. "New Religious Cults in Japan," *Hibbert Journal,* LX (July 1962), pp. 305–313. A good first article to read, discussing the origins of the New Religions in folk religion and popular religion.

Earhart, H. Byron. "The Interpretation of the 'New Religions' of Japan as Historical Phenomena," *Journal of the American Academy of Religion,* XXXVII, No. 3 (September 1969), pp. 237–48. Treats the origin and nature of the New Religions within the context of Japanese religious history.

―――――. "The Interpretation of the 'New Religions' of Japan as New Religious Movements," in *Religious Ferment in Asia.* Edited by Robert J. Miller. Lawrence, Kansas: The University Press of Kansas, forthcoming. Treats the New Religions comparatively and theoretically in relation to similar movements in other geographical areas.

―――――. "The Significance of the 'New Religions' for Understanding Japanese Religion," *KBS Bulletin on Japanese Culture,* CI (April–May 1970), pp. 1–9. A general discussion of the New Religions in terms of six persistent themes in Japanese religion.

Fujiwara, Hirotatsu. *I Denounce Soka Gakkai.* Translated by Worth C. Grant. Tokyo: Nishin Hodo Co., 1970. A polemical work; alleged suppression of the Japanese edition of this book was the cause of a public scandal investigation by the National Diet.

Ikado, Fujio. "Trend and Problems of New Religions: Religion in Urban Society." In *The Sociology of Japanese Religion,* pp. 101–17. Edited by Kiyomi Morioka and William H. Newell. Leiden: E. J. Brill, 1968. Analysis of statistical and sociological information about the membership of the New Religions in the postwar urban setting.

*McFarland, H. Neill. *The Rush Hour of the Gods. A Study of the New Religious Movements in Japan.* New York: The Macmillan Company, 1967. A general account of five New Religions.

Murata, Kiyoaki. *Japan's New Buddhism. An Objective Account of Soka Gakkai.* New York and Tokyo: Walker/Weatherhill, 1969. A general introduction based mainly on the publications of Soka Gakkai.

The Nichiren Shoshu Sokagakkai. Tokyo: The Seikyo Press, 1966. A publication by this organization about its philosophy of life, activities, and goals.

Offner, Clark B., and Straelen, Henry van. *Modern Japanese Religions, With Special Emphasis Upon Their Doctrines of Healing.* Tokyo: Rupert Enderle, 1963. A brief treatment of Tenrikyo and seven other groups, focusing on healing techniques, by two Christian missionaries.

Plath, David W. "The Fate of Utopia: Adaptive Tactics in Four Japanese Groups," *American Anthropologist,* LXVIII, Pt. 2 (1966), pp. 1152–62. Analyzes the attempt of four communal groups to achieve utopian alternatives to the dilemmas of modernization.

A Short History of Tenrikyo. Tenri, Japan: Tenrikyo Kyokai Honbu, 1956. Published by Tenrikyo headquarters, it includes chapters on the life of the foundress, the history of the movement, and its activities.

Straelen, Henry van. *The Religion of Divine Wisdom. Japan's Most Powerful Movement.* Kyoto: Veritas Shoin, 1957 (and later editions). The most complete account of Tenrikyo by a Western scholar.

Sugihara, Yoshie, and Plath, David W. *Sensei and His People. The Building of a Japanese Commune.* Berkeley and Los Angeles: University of California Press, 1969. An interesting firsthand account of the development of a communal group, partly an offshoot of Tenrikyo, by the second wife of the founder.

White, James W. *The Sokagakkai and Mass Society.* Stanford: Stanford University Press, 1970. A technical study, utilizing contemporary social science theory for the most complete behavioral analysis of Soka Gakkai in English.

Index

Japanese names are cited in the text in Japanese fashion, with family name first, such as Tokugawa Ieyasu. The family name is Tokugawa, and will be found in the index under Tokugawa. In order to simplify use of the index, English equivalents are given for some Japanese and other foreign-language terms. Many religious terms have been grouped under the religion of which they are a part, such as Buddhism, Shinto, or Christianity.

INDEX

Index 147